Illustrated
English Idioms Book 1

GlobalELT
ENGLISH LANGUAGE TEACHING BOOKS

Preface

An idiom is an **expression**, a colloquial metaphor, which has a figurative meaning that is known only through common use. The meaning of this phrase or expression cannot be deduced by finding the meaning of each individual word.

Idioms are considered part of the culture of a language and, in order to be understood, they require some knowledge, information, or experience that the members of this culture share. It is believed that William Shakespeare coined over 2,000 idioms that are still in use today.

Example: *e.g. If you finish your lessons, you can come with me;* **_the ball's in your court_** *now.*

In the English language expression: *the ball's in your court now,* a non-native speaker would be unable to deduce the actual meaning of this phrase, which has nothing to do with sports and it is used to show that somebody is responsible for the **next move in a situation**. Although it can refer literally to sports/tennis, it is rarely used in that way. Also, it cannot always be directly translated to other languages because it might have a completely different meaning. However, some idioms can be found in many different languages and they can be easily translated, or their metaphorical meaning can be easily deduced.

Idioms are very important in English and quite difficult for students to learn. Students have to learn idiomatic expressions the way they learn other vocabulary. Some of the most common ones that students will come across are dealt with in this book.

Some things to keep in mind about idioms are:
a) The meaning of an idiom cannot be deduced by a literal translation of its spare words.
b) We cannot substitute a word in an idiom with a word similar in meaning.
c) We cannot usually modify an idiomatic phrase syntactically.

This book aims to build up students' knowledge of English Idioms through full-colour illustrations, which are accompanied by graded exercises. Throughout each unit, the new Idioms introduced are recycled, and students are exposed to every new Idiom on seven (7) different occasions.

There are also 2 Revision Tests (**RT1**: *Units 1-5* and **RT2**: *Units 6-10*) which also revise and consolidate the English Idioms that students have already been taught.

The book is intended for intermediate/upper- intermediate level students (**B1** and **B2**), or even more advanced students (**IELTS** Score: *from 5.0 up to 7.0*) who want to practise or revise their knowledge of this area of the language. It can be used in the classroom, or for self-study purposes. The exercises can be given as homework and then discussed in class.

Published by
GLOBAL ELT LTD
www.globalelt.co.uk
Copyright © **GLOBAL ELT LTD, 2012**

British Library Cataloguing-in-Publication Data
A catalogue record of this book is available from the British Library.

● ILLUSTRATED ENGLISH IDIOMS - Levels: B1 & B2 TEACHER'S BOOK **ISBN:** 978-1-904663-32-4
● ILLUSTRATED ENGLISH IDIOMS - Levels: B1 & B2 STUDENT'S BOOK **ISBN:** 978-1-904663-31-7

Contents

Illustrated English Idioms

The structure of each Unit:

The Idioms are presented with their definitions at the beginning of the unit.

Full-colour illustrations show what each Idiom means, accompanied by <u>Activity A</u> (matching / gap-filling).

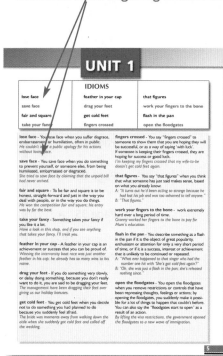

A variety of exercises (Activities B, C and D) help students master the use of the most frequent English Idioms.

A fun activity for revising the Idioms is provided at the end of each unit.

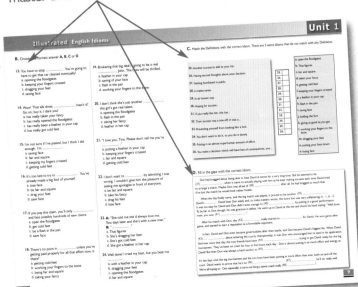

UNIT 1

IDIOMS

lose face	**feather in your cap**	**that figures**
save face	drag your feet	work your fingers to the bone
fair and square	**get cold feet**	**flash in the pan**
take your fancy	fingers crossed	open the floodgates

lose face - You lose face when you suffer disgrace, embarrassment or humiliation, often in public.
He couldn't issue a public apology for his actions without losing face.

save face - You save face when you do something to prevent yourself, or someone else, from being humiliated, embarrassed or disgraced.
She tried to save face by claiming that the unpaid bill had never arrived.

fair and square - To be fair and square is to be honest, straight-forward and just in the way you deal with people, or in the way you do things.
He won the competition fair and square; his entry was by far the best.

take your fancy - Something takes your fancy if you like it a lot.
Have a look in this shop, and if you see anything that takes your fancy, I'll treat you.

feather in your cap - A feather in your cap is an achievement or success that you can be proud of.
Winning the intervarsity boat race was just another feather in his cap; he already has so many wins to his name.

drag your feet - If you do something very slowly, or delay doing something, because you don't really want to do it, you are said to be dragging your feet.
The management have been dragging their feet over giving us our holiday bonuses.

get cold feet - You get cold feet when you decide not to do something you had planned to do because you suddenly feel afraid.
The bride was moments away from walking down the aisle when she suddenly got cold feet and called off the wedding.

fingers crossed - You say "fingers crossed" to someone to show them that you are hoping they will be successful, or as a way of saying 'with luck'.
If someone is keeping their fingers crossed, they are hoping for success or good luck.
I'm keeping my fingers crossed that my wife-to-be doesn't get cold feet again.

that figures - You say "that figures" when you think that what someone has just said makes sense, based on what you already know.
A: "It turns out he'd been acting so strange because he had lost his job and was too ashamed to tell anyone."
B: "That figures."

work your fingers to the bone - work extremely hard over a long period of time.
Granny worked her fingers to the bone to pay for Mum's education.

flash in the pan - You describe something as a flash in the pan if it is the object of great popularity, enthusiasm or attention for only a very short period of time, or if it is a success, interest or achievement that is unlikely to be continued or repeated.
A: "What ever happened to that singer who had the number one hit with 'She's got cold feet again'?"
B: "Oh, she was just a flash in the pan; she's released nothing since."

open the floodgates - You open the floodgates when you remove restrictions or controls that have been repressing thoughts, feelings or actions; by opening the floodgates, you suddenly make it possible for a lot of things to happen that couldn't before. You can also say the "floodgates start to open" as a result of an action.
By lifting the visa restrictions, the government opened the floodgates to a new wave of immigration.

A. Fill in the gaps in the sentences below with the correct Idiom from Unit 1.

1. The public nature of their disagreement meant that everybody in the room would ...lose face... .

4. **A:** "He's so confident and he really loves himself - he's a politician you know." **B:** "...That figures...!"

2. Max was keeping his ...fingers crossed.... that the bank manager would approve his loan application.

5. Matt knew he couldn't surf to save his life, but he was able to ...save face... by inventing an ingenious new board design !

3. Bob added ...a feather in his cap... by winning the basketball championship. Better still; he was team captain and got to keep the trophy for a year.

6. John knew he eventually had to decide whether or not to say yes to Kate's marriage proposal, but because he liked the free life, he was ...dragging his feet... .

7. Although Betty was upset, she knew Deborah and Tim had won the dance-off ..fair and square.. .

10. That lady in the pink skirt really ..took.. John's ..fancy.. ! takes
I bet he's going to hire her!

8. As Prof. Dun began explaining yet another theory, Mark started to get ..cold feet.. about his decision to become a maths teacher.

11. While mum ..worked her fingers to the bone.. doing the house-work; dad just sat on the sofa each night and never lent a hand.

9. Nora's obsession with golf turned out to be just another ..flash in the pan..; a month later and she is sick of it already!

12. By asking if anyone had any questions, he ..opened the.. ..floodgates.. and spent the next two hours being quizzed!

B. Choose the correct answer **A, B, C** or **D**.

13. You have to stop .... You're going to have to get that car cleaned eventually!
    a. opening the floodgates
    b. keeping your fingers crossed
    c. dragging your feet
    d. saving face

14. Wow! That silk dress .... , hasn't it? Go on; buy it. I dare you!
    a. has really taken your fancy
    b. has really opened the floodgates
    c. has really been a feather in your cap
    d. has really got cold feet

15. I'm not sure if I've passed, but I think I did enough. I'm ....
    a. saving face
    b. fair and square
    c. keeping my fingers crossed
    d. getting cold feet

16. It's too late to try to .... You've already made a big fool of yourself.
    a. lose face
    b. be fair and square
    c. drag your feet
    d. save face

17. If you pay this claim, you'll only .... and face possibly hundreds of new claims.
    a. open the floodgates
    b. get cold feet
    c. be a flash in the pan
    d. save face

18. There's no point in .... unless you're getting paid properly for all that effort now, is there?
    a. getting cold feet
    b. working your fingers to the bone
    c. being fair and square
    d. taking your fancy

19. Brokering that big deal is going to be a real .... , John. The boss will be thrilled.
    a. feather in your cap
    b. saving of your face
    c. flash in the pan
    d. working your fingers to the bone

20. I don't think she's just another .... ; this girl's got real talent.
    a. opening the floodgates
    b. flash in the pan
    c. taking her fancy
    d. feather in her cap

21. "I love you, Tina. Please don't tell me you're ...."
    a. putting a feather in your cap
    b. keeping your fingers crossed
    c. fair and square
    d. getting cold feet

22. I don't want to .... by admitting I was wrong. I wouldn't give him the pleasure of seeing me apologise in front of everyone.
    a. be fair and square
    b. take his fancy
    c. drag his feet
    d. lose face

23. **A:** "She told me she'd always love me. Two days later and she's with a new man."
    B: "................... ."
    a. That figures
    b. She's dragging her feet
    c. She's got cold feet
    d. She got a feather in her cap

24. Well done! I tried my best, but you beat me ....
    a. with a feather in your cap
    b. dragging your feet
    c. opening the floodgates
    d. fair and square

C. Match the Definitions with the correct Idiom. There are 3 extra Idioms that do not match with any Definition.

25. Another success to add to your list.

26. Having second thoughts about your decision.

27. Getting humiliated in public.

28. It makes sense.

29. In an honest way.

30. Hoping for success.

31. If you really like her, she has...

32. Their success was a one-off; it was a...

33. Preventing yourself from looking like a fool.

34. You don't want to do it, so you do it slowly.

35. Putting in an almost superhuman amount of effort.

36. You make a decision which will have lots of consequences, you...

25.	g
26.	e
27.	o
28.	b
29.	c
30.	f
31.	d
32.	h
33.	i
34.	m
35.	l
36.	a

a. open the floodgates

b. That figures.

c. fair and square

d. taken your fancy

e. getting cold feet

f. keeping your fingers crossed

g. a feather in your cap

h. flash in the pan

i. saving face

j. holding the fort

k. giving as good as you get

l. working your fingers to the bone

m. dragging your feet

n. putting your foot down

o. losing face

D. Fill in the gaps with the correct Idiom.

Don had bragged about being able to beat David at tennis for a very long time. But he seemed to be (37) ...dragging his feet... when it came to actually playing with him as he kept making excuses each time David tried to arrange a match. Maybe Don was afraid of (38) ...losing face... ; after all, he had bragged so much that if he lost the match he would look rather foolish.

When the day finally came, and the big match was played, it proved to be another (39) ...feather in... David's ...cap... . David beat Don easily and, to make matters worse, the score line was very unflattering; 6 - 1, 6 - 3. It was too easy for David and Don didn't even manage to (40) ...save face... by putting in a good performance. To be fair to Don though, he was gracious in defeat. He went up to David at the net and shook his hand saying: "Well done mate, you won (41) ...fair and square...".

After his match with Don, the (42) ...floodgates... really started to ...open... for David. He won game after game, and started to earn a reputation as a formidable opponent.

In fact, David and Don even became great buddies after their battle, and Don became David's biggest fan. When David (43) ...got cold feet... about entering the county championship, it was Don who encouraged him to send in his application. And ever since that day, the two friends have been (44)...working their fingers to the bone trying to get David ready for the big tournament. They've been on court for four to five hours each day - Don is almost putting in as much effort and energy as David! But then Don was always a hard worker so (45) ...that figures... .

It's ten days until the big tournament and the two boys have been putting in more effort than ever, both on and off the court. David wants to prove that he's no (46) ...flash in the pan... . (47) ...Fingers crossed... , he'll do really well. We're all hoping so - Don especially; it turns out being a tennis coach really (48) ...takes his fancy... !

E. Do the CrossWord Puzzle, finding the correct IDIOM from Unit 1..

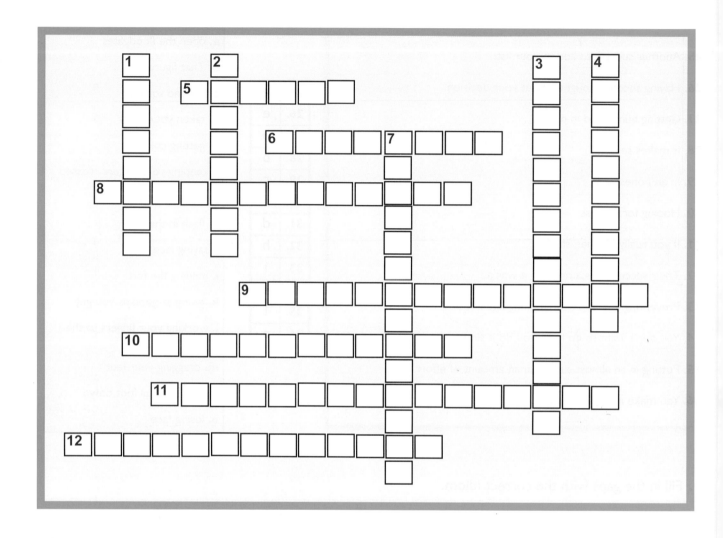

ACROSS

5. Once she admitted how hard it's been for her, the floodgates started ....to open............... and she broke into tears.

6. I'm a little afraid she won't go through with it; what if she gets ....cold feet............. ?

8. They had better players, but we had a better team spirit - we won ......fair and square............. .

9. I really think that, if we perform well, we can win - ......fingers crossed......... !

10. That new shirt you have really ....takes my fancy............. .

11. Stop .....dragging your feet.... and get on with it!

12. Oh, don't worry. She's young; every idea she gets is just another ....flash in the pan........... .

DOWN

1. How dare you question me in front of my parents like that? You're just lucky I was able to ....save face..........!

2. I was so pleased to see that James fellow put in his place by Thomas; he's so arrogant and I didn't feel a bit sorry for him and his 'public' embarrassment. I'm glad he ......lost face......... .

3. You ungrateful little brat; your dad and I have ...worked our fingers... to the bone to pay for your college education.

4. ....That figures............. ; I always knew he was a quitter. I'm not a bit surprised he gave up.

7. It's not like I have to win this competition; I've won so many already, so this would be another feather in my cap .

UNIT 2

IDIOMS

give as good as you get	(not) let the grass grow under your feet	fools rush in
up to no good	grin and bear it	put your foot down
make the grade	a fool and his money are soon parted	a frog in your throat
the grass is always greener on the other side	get off on the wrong foot	hold the fort

give as good as you get -
You give as good as you get when you fight, argue or joke with other people just as well as they fight, argue or joke with you.
Don't worry about Kate; she's able to take care of herself; she can give as good as she gets.

up to no good - Someone who is up to no good is secretly doing something dishonest or illegal.
If you ask me, he's up to no good; look how suspiciously he's acting.

make the grade - You make tha grade when you reach the required standard.
Determination and resilience are two of the most important qualities needed to make the grade as a sportsperson.

the grass is always greener on the other side -
If you say that "the grass is always greener on the other side" you mean that things that you don't have, or cannot have, always seem more attractive than the things that you do have.
John was never happy no matter what he had; to him, the grass was always greener on the other side.

(not) let the grass grow under your feet -
You do not let the grass grow under your feet when you do not delay, or waste time.
Get on with it you lot; don't let the grass grow under your feet.

grin and bear it -
You have to grin and bear it when you have to tolerate an unpleasant situation because you have no choice.
I'm in a dead-end job, but for the moment I'm just going to have to grin and bear it as I've got no other options.

a fool and his money are soon parted -
A fool and his money are soon parted means that you are foolish if you spend money too quickly, rather than save it. It also means people who are foolish will not keep their money for long.
A: *"Did you hear about the lotto winner who blew all his winnings gambling in Las Vegas?"*
B: *"Well, you know what they say: 'a fool and his money are soon parted'!"*

get off on the wrong foot - You get off on the wrong foot when you start something badly; if you get off on the wrong foot with a person, you don't make a good first impression on them.
A: *"How did you get on with his parents?"*
B: *"Well, I got off on the wrong foot with them by using their first names."*

fools rush in - If you say fools rush in, you mean that foolish people attempt to do things without thinking about the consequences; things that wiser people would avoid.
He volunteered to take a class of 35 kids camping; now there's a case of 'fools rush in'!

put your foot down - To decide very firmly not to allow something to happen; to put your foot down is to be strict.
You're going to have to put your foot down this time; you can't let the children go out late at night.

a frog in your throat -
You say you've got a frog in your throat if your voice is not clear, and you feel like you need to cough.
Excuse me, ehe ehem..., I've got a bit of a frog in my throat.

hold the fort - You hold the fort when you temporarily take over the running of an organization for someone who is absent for a short period.
A: *"Where's Mrs McLeod?"*
B: *"She's on holiday; I'm holding the fort."*

Illustrated English Idioms

A. Fill in the gaps in the sentences below with the correct Idiom from Unit 2.

1. Nancy might have been the butt of some jokes, but she was able to ....give as good as she got....... .

2. I'm so happy I've been accepted into music school; I finally ...made the grade............. .

3. Jane is forever busy, and you know there's no way this girl will ...let the grass grow under her feet... .

4. Only after he'd knocked down the tree did John realise it was the wrong one. You know what they say: '....fools rush in.....'.

5. Billy lives in a mansion, but he says he'd like to live in a cottage better; ..the grass is always greener on the other side.. !

6. Uhh! I hope I can manage to ......grin and bear... this horrible job for another six weeks until I get my Christmas bonus.

12

7. Alex spent money as though it grew on trees and in a few months he was broke; 'a fool and his money are soon parted '.

10. Tina was worried that her parents might find out she was up to no good............ and be angry with her.

8. The kids are being allowed to do whatever they want; you're going to have to ..put your foot down.. with them.

11. Everything was going fine until Anna pointed at Toby's bald head - talk about getting off on the wrong foot !

9. Now I really wish I hadn't done so much screaming at the concert; I've ..got a frog in my throat.......... .

12. Michael did a great job ....holding the fort...... for Jane while she was away on holidays.

B. Choose the correct answer **A**, **B**, **C** or **D**.

13. Look, I don't want to .... with you; let's be friends.
    a. give as good as I get
    b. make the grade
    c. get off on the wrong foot
    d. grin and bear it

14. No matter how hard I study, I just don't think I will be able to .... It's too difficult.
    a. grin and bear it
    b. make the grade
    c. put my foot down
    d. give as good as I get

15. Right! That's it; I'm .... ; stop that horrible screaming and shouting this instant or else!'
    a. putting my foot down
    b. not letting the grass grow under my feet
    c. getting off on the wrong foot
    d. holding the fort

16. **A:** "How do you put up with your brother's teasing?"
    B: "I just have to ...."
    a. make the grade
    b. hold the fort
    c. grin and bear it
    d. get off on the wrong foot

17. **A:** "Do you think Emma will be OK with all those girls at camp? They're older than her."
    B: "Don't you worry love, Emma can ...."
    a. give as good as she gets
    b. get off on the wrong foot
    c. have a frog in her throat
    d. hold the fort

18. I'll be back in about half an hour; can you .... while I'm gone?
    a. grin and bear it
    b. hold the fort
    c. give as good as you get
    d. get off on the wrong foot

19. I got a call from Emma's teacher again today; she's been .... doing mischief as usual.
    a. holding the fort
    b. rushing in like a fool
    c. grinning and bearing it
    d. up to no good

20. **A:** "She's so lucky to be single and carefree."
    B: "She probably thinks you're lucky to be engaged; ...."
    a. the grass is always greener on the other side
    b. only fools rush in
    c. a fool and her money are soon parted
    d. don't let the grass grow under your feet

21. Come along, let's keep moving; we've got a lot to do. We haven't got time to ....
    a. let the grass grow under our feet
    b. hold the fort
    c. get off on the wrong foot
    d. put our feet down

22. **A:** "John, why do you think that ex-millionaire ended up living on the street?"
    B: "It's quite simple dear: ...."
    a. he got off on the wrong foot
    b. a fool and his money are soon parted
    c. fools rush in
    d. you have to give as good as you get

23. **A:** "I can't understand a thing you said."
    B: "Sorry, I've ...."
    a. been up to no good
    b. got a frog in my throat
    c. put my foot down
    d. held the fort

24. Emma, you've only known him for four weeks; don't talk about marriage yet; ....
    a. only fools rush in
    b. give as good as you get
    c. make the grade
    d. grin and bear it

C. Match the Definitions with the correct Idiom. There are 3 extra Idioms that do not match with any Definition.

25. You can stand up for yourself and defend yourself. You can...

26. Always misbehaving.

27. Achieve the target or the standard.

28. What other people have, always looks better than what you have.

29. Don't waste time; don't...

30. It's a difficult situation, but you can't change it. You've got to...

31. Some people can't manage their finances properly and always seem to have no money, which just proves...

32. To upset someone the first time you meet them.

33. Some people don't think before acting and make big mistakes as a result.

34. To decide to be very strict.

35. You can't speak clearly because you have...

36. To take charge while someone else is away for a short amount of time.

25.	l
26.	f
27.	c
28.	g
29.	h
30.	i
31.	a
32.	j
33.	o
34.	m
35.	b
36.	k

a. a fool and his money are soon parted

b. a frog in your throat

c. make the grade

d. hand in glove

e. work your guts out

f. up to no good

g. the grass is always greener on the other side

h. let the grass grow under your feet

i. grin and bear it

j. get off on the wrong foot

k. hold the fort

l. give as good as you get

m. put your foot down

n. an old hand

o. fools rush in

D. Fill in the gaps with the correct Idiom.

John might look weak, but don't be fooled; he can **(37)** give as good as he gets . The only character flaw he has, if you ask me, is that in his eyes everyone else has it better than him. Yes, **(38)** the grass is always greener on the other side as far as John is concerned. That said though, he's not afraid of hard work, and he never fails to **(39)** make the grade ; John will succeed in anything you ask of him. Last year, when Jenny was out on maternity leave, he **(40)** held the fort for her. In fact, when Jenny came back, she admitted the business was in a better state than ever thanks to John's endeavours.

And that's another thing - his hard work ethic means that he is never prepared to waste time; John will never **(41)** let the grass grow under his feet , that's for sure! He hates play-acting and he used to get angry with the staff when they started messing around. It's not that they were **(42)** up to no good ; it was just harmless fun, but even still, John wasn't prepared to stand for it. He shouted at them so much while Jenny was away that he ended up with **(43)** a frog in the/his throat ; poor John! But, in fairness, the fact that he **(44)** put his foot down and was so strict might explain why everyone performed well. One thing's for sure though, he certainly **(45)** got off on the wrong foot with the rest of the staff. At the start, they hated him; he was such a slave driver! But eventually they got to like him and saw that he meant well, and was honest and sincere. Well, apart from Michael. Michael and John never got on. But John was the boss, so Michael had to **(46)** grin and bear it . If he didn't like John's decisions, that was tough luck! Michael placed a bet with the other staff members that John would give up and leave within the first week. Needless to say, he didn't and Michael lost a lot of money on that bet! But then I suppose **(47)** a fool and his money are soon parted ! Michael was pretty bitter after that, and the next time Jenny needed a few days off, he volunteered to take charge - but he didn't really think about what he was volunteering for. Michael couldn't handle the stress and half an hour into his first day he was on the phone to John looking for help! He soon learned his lesson - only **(48)** fools rush in - maybe he'll think about it more carefully before he volunteers again next time!

E. Do the CrossWord Puzzle, finding the correct IDIOM from Unit 2.

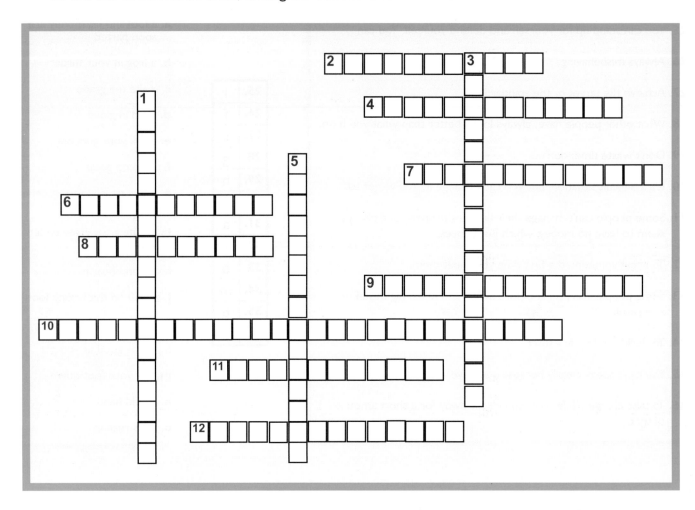

ACROSS

2. Would you be able to ....hold the fort.......................... while I'm away next month?

4. You know what they say about a fool and his money; they ....are soon parted.......................... .

6. Only ....fools rush in.......................... ; take your time and make the right decision.

7. We all go through a bad period in life sometimes; you've just got to ...grin and bear it.................., I'm afraid.

8. Why are you being so secretive? Are you ....up to no good........... again?

9. Look, just try to stay busy; do ....not let the grass....... grow under those feet of yours whatever you do, okay?

10. Oh, stop complaining! You know what they say about that grass; it's ....always greener on the other side.... .

11. I believe in you; work hard and I know you can ....make the grade........ .

12. That was an awful first date; talk about getting off .....on the wrong foot.......... .

DOWN

1. What I like about you is that, although people sometimes make fun of you, you ......give as good as you get............ .

3. I can't understand a word you're saying; have you got a ....frog in your throat.......... or something?

5. You're too easy on the children; you have to know when to .....put your foot down.............. !

UNIT 3

IDIOMS

give someone a free hand	win hands down	break new ground
old hand	hand in glove	work your guts out
on hand	get to grips with	keep your hair on
have your hands full	hold your ground	have the guts to do something

give someone a free hand -
Let someone organise something their own way, rather than supervise them yourself; when you let them do things whatever way they want to
I'm putting my trust in you - I believe you can do this by yourself, so I'm giving you a free hand.

old hand - You describe someone as an old hand at something if they have been doing it for a long time and know how to do it well.
I was becoming an old hand at presenting; I wasn't nearly as nervous this time, even though the audience was twice the size.

on hand - You have someone on hand if they are present in case they are needed.
John is always on hand if you have trouble with your computer.

have your hands full - To be very busy.
And Mother had her hands full coping with the housework and holding down a full-time job, too.

win hands down - Beat someone or win something very easily.
When we had a quiz, Ken always won hands down - no one could compete with him.

hand in glove - To be closely associated with someone; two things are hand in glove with one another if they have a close relationship. The verbs 'work' and 'go' may be used with this phrase.
Happiness and having a good, stable personal life go hand in glove.

get to grips with - You get to grips with a subject, for example, when you start understanding it or being able to deal with it. You get to grips with a situation when you get it under control.
I've never really been into that kind of poetry; I can't get to grips with it.

hold your ground -
Argue for something you believe without being intimidated or easily persuaded by other people's arguments. To defend yourself.
I had to fight for what I believe in, so I held my ground.

break new ground -
Discover or invent something new. Something breaks new ground when it is very innovative and does things that were never done before.
Far from breaking new ground, most of the designs bear a strong relation to that which has gone before.

work your guts out - Work very hard.
I worked my guts out getting my doctorate, and look where it's got me!

keep your hair on - Calm down
All right, all right! Keep your hair on! Don't panic!

have the guts to do something -
If you have the guts to do something, you are not afraid to do it; you have the courage to do it.
He was the only one who had the guts to say what he really thought.

A. Fill in the gaps in the sentences below with the correct Idiom from Unit 3.

1. Poor grandad never really ......*got to grips with*..... the idea of how to deal with lots of little children at the same time.

4. During her first performance, she was terribly nervous, but now she performs like an ....*old hand*................ .

2. I don't know what I would have done if you weren't here; it's lucky you were .....*on hand*.............. .

5. Poor Betty really ....*has her hands full*...... looking after two children and trying to do all the household chores, too.

3. What a performance by this sensational golfer; she has ..*won hands down*.......... . No one can get close to her!

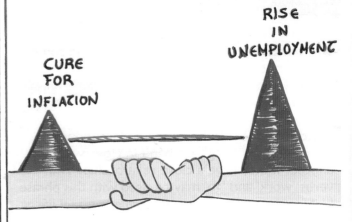

6. Isn't it funny how a rise in unemployment provides a cure for inflation? The two go .....*hand in glove*............ .

7. I ...gave... Paul .....a free hand..... to organise the staff party and he's been on his phone all day trying to find a venue.

10. I don't care what he says; I am going to win this debate by ..holding my ground and sticking up for what I believe in.

8. I don't think the artist ..broke new ground with this picture. At least, I don't think it's very clever or innovative.

11. I think you've had one too many coffees, Tina. Relax and .keep your hair on We still have 3 hours before the exam.

9. Well, he finally .....had the guts to...........ask her out. Unfortunately, she turned him down!

12. He has spoken to over ten thousand people trying to raise money for this charity. He really has .worked his guts out .

B. Choose the correct answer **A, B, C** or **D**.

13. Wow, that's impressive. How did you become so good at this so quickly? You're almost ....
    a. holding your ground
    b. on hand
    c. hand in glove
    d. like an old hand

14. **A:** "What's the matter, love?"
    B: "Well, here I am .... while you lie on the sofa all day!"
    a. winning hands down
    b. keeping my hair on
    c. breaking new ground
    d. working my guts out

15. It's a sad state of affairs, but it's true; politics and corruption seem to .... these days.
    a. work hand in glove
    b. give people a free hand
    c. win hands down
    d. hold their ground

16. John gallantly climbed up to rescue the kitten; lucky he was .... !
    a. working his guts out
    b. on hand
    c. holding his ground
    d. winning hands down

17. Sorry Nancy, I can't make it to the theatre tonight; John's taken ill so I .... looking after the kids.
    a. gave him a free hand
    b. won hands down
    c. have my hands full
    d. worked hand in glove

18. Alright, there's no need to start screaming and shouting; ....
    a. keep your hair on
    b. work your guts out
    c. act like an old hand
    d. give him a free hand

19. I've been up all night studying for this maths exam, but I just can't seem to ....
    a. have my hands full
    b. work my guts out
    c. keep my hair on
    d. get to grips with it

20. Ha ha! Got you! That's three games in a row; I ....
    a. hold my ground
    b. am on hand
    c. win hands down
    d. work my guts out

21. Don't go anywhere; .... ; this is a peaceful protest and we have a right to be here.
    a. hold your ground
    b. have your hands full
    c. work your guts out
    d. work hand in glove

22. Why did you go and .... ? I don't trust him and there's no telling what he'll do.
    a. work your guts out
    b. keep your hair on
    c. get to grips with it
    d. give him a free hand

23. Wow, that new product is just amazing; look at all the things it can do - talk about ....
    a. breaking new ground
    b. working hand in glove
    c. having your hands full
    d. getting to grips with it

24. Sally is too shy to speak in front of so many people; there's no way she'd ....
    a. have the guts to do it
    b. have her hands full
    c. give them a free hand
    d. break new ground

C. Match the Definitions with the correct IDIOM. There are 3 extra Idioms that do not match with any Definition.

25. Someone very skilled and experienced at doing something.

26. Allow someone to have total responsibility for the running of something.

27. Show the courage to get something done.

28. Don't panic.

29. Try extremely hard to achieve something.

30. If you are doing lots of different tasks at the same time, you...

31. You get an easy victory; you...

32. If something is new and innovative, it's going to...

33. When two things have a very close relationship, they work...

34. Learn to deal with something.

35. Defend your point of view.

36. Ready and willing to help.

25.	c
26.	o
27.	h
28.	g
29.	m
30.	i
31.	d
32.	f
33.	a
34.	l
35.	e
36.	k

a. hand in glove
b. lending a hand
c. an old hand
d. win hands down
e. hold your ground
f. break new ground
g. keep your hair on
h. have the guts to do it
i. have your hands full
j. no kidding
k. on hand
l. get to grips with it
m. work your guts out
n. hit the jackpot
o. give them a free hand

D. Fill in the gaps with the correct Idiom.

The biggest mistake I ever made was to give gran (37) a free hand with the children. I figured: "she's (38) an old hand so she'll know what to do", but I couldn't have been more wrong! In a battle of wits today between kids and old people, the kids will (39) win hands down; they're so street-smart that poor gran didn't stand a chance! Needless to say, she (40) had her hands full trying to keep control of my lot of little brats! In fact, she couldn't (41) get to grips with the situation at all. Luckily, my sister Rebecca was (42) on hand to help, otherwise there would have been total mayhem. When she arrived, the kids were jumping around on the sofa, having pillowcase fights, shouting and screaming. But Rebecca's way of dealing with the kids was absolutely brilliant - she (43) broke new ground in terms of parenting skills, if you ask me.

First, she walked straight past and ignored the kids in order to deal with poor gran. She told gran to (44) keep her hair on and relax; she was there now and she would deal with the situation. For a moment, gran (45) held her ground and said everything was under control; that she could deal with the situation by herself - gran's very proud! But eventually she backed down and allowed Rebecca to take control.

Meanwhile, the kids were just ignoring everything that was going on, and they were half expecting Rebecca to yell at them to be quiet or something - which, of course, would have done no good at all. But Rebecca didn't yell; she just sat herself down in front of the T.V. and said nothing - she was totally quiet. "Aunty Becca", said Jenny (my eldest daughter), "what's wrong?" - still not a sound from Rebecca.

This went on for a half hour until the kids finally started to get worried. In Rebecca's silence and in their confusion, they were afraid. Then something amazing happened; they started to clean up all by themselves. I'd never have believed it! They (46) worked their guts out and, by the time I came home, the place was spotless. Rebecca's scheme had worked perfectly, but I still can't believe she (47) had the guts to do it. Bravo Aunty Becca! Now I've learned that silence and good parenting go (48) hand in glove. It's great - I'll never have to raise my voice again!

E. Do the CrossWord Puzzle, finding the correct IDIOM from Unit 3.

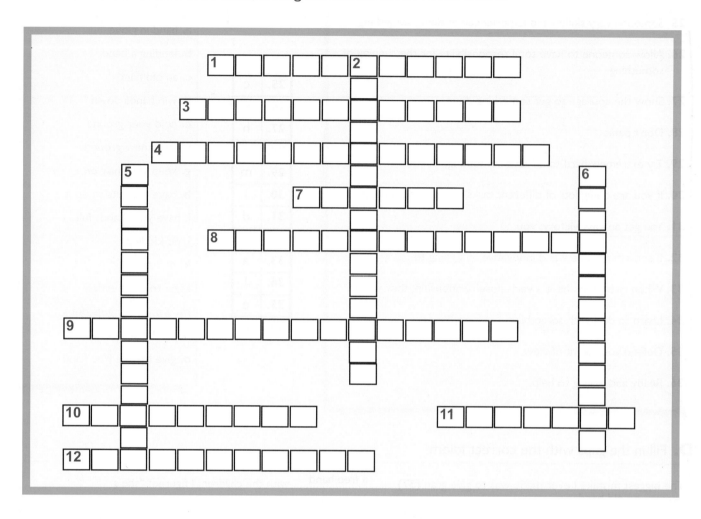

ACROSS

1. I don't think I would ...... have the guts ...... to do a bungee jump; I'd be terrified!

3. At the end of the contest, all the judges chose him as the winner; he ...... won hands down ....

4. It took me all night, but I finally ...... got to grips with ...... the chemistry questions our teacher set for homework.

7. It's nice to know that if I ever need you, you are always ...... on hand ....

8. Last month, our innovative method of disposing of waste material ...... broke new ground ....

9. Although she ...... worked her guts out ...... for six weeks coming up to the exam, she still failed.

10. You're not going to get given ...... a free hand ...... ; I will be keeping an eye on you at all times.

11. That's impressive! I should have known to leave it to the ...... old hand ...... - you've shown us how it's done!

12. In business, a good reputation and good customer service go ...... hand in glove ...... as far as I'm concerned.

DOWN

2. He ...... had his hands full ...... trying to cope with his work and looking after his sick grandfather, too.

5. ...... Keep your hair on ...... Ashling! You know I'm busy. I'll be with you in a minute.

6. She was convinced she was right, so she ...... held her ground ...... and wouldn't change her position no matter what anyone said.

UNIT 4

IDIOMS

give 'em an inch and they'll take a mile	**take a joke**	**of a kind**
hit the jackpot	for a start	the kiss of death
make the best of a bad job	**no kidding?**	**under the knife**
beyond a joke	a/some kind of	bring someone to their knees

give 'em (them) an inch and they'll take a mile - "Give 'em an inch and they'll take a mile" means that if you do a small favour for a particular person or group of people, they will take advantage of your kindness and demand more.
A: *"I told him he could go home early on Friday to watch the match, but now he's started leaving early every day with one excuse or another"*
B: *"Typical; give 'em an inch and they'll take a mile."*

hit the jackpot - Win or obtain a lot of money or success.
Unemployed road sweeper Mickey Reid hit the jackpot when his $4 lottery ticket won him $1.8 million.

make the best of a bad job - Do your best to make an unpleasant situation as pleasant or as tolerable as possible.
Okay, so the weather's terrible, but why don't we just make the best of a bad job and book into a nice hotel for the night?

beyond a joke - Something is beyond a joke when it has become unacceptable, or when it has become very serious or intolerable.
The noise coming from the flat next door is getting beyond a joke. What are we going to do about it?

take a joke - Someone who can take a joke is able to laugh at jokes that other people make about them.
Oh, come on! You know I didn't mean it when I said you were a baby. Can't you take a joke?

for a start - You say "for a start" to emphasise that what you are saying is just the first in a list of arguments or complaints.
"What's wrong?" " Well, I don't feel great for a start ... and I had a bit of bad news this morning."

no kidding? - You say "no kidding?" to someone when they have just said something surprising, and you are checking that it is true.
A: *"My dad knew Elvis Presley before he was famous."*
B: *"No kidding?"*

a/some kind of - You use "a/some kind of" when giving a rough description or idea of something.
The pudding was a kind of cheesecakey thing, but without a cheesecake-base.

of a kind - You say that a small number of people or objects are two, three, etc, of a kind if they are the same as or similar to one another.
In the card game cribbage, three of a kind (three kings, for example) gives you six points.

the kiss of death - An action someone does which is meant to be helpful to another person, but which in fact does them a lot of harm. You can also say that an action or result is the kiss of death if it causes disaster or misfortune for someone or a group of people.
A reference from your boss would be the kiss of death. I mean it; everyone in the business hates him.

under the knife - You say that someone is going under the knife when they are going to have an operation; when they are going for surgery.
I go into hospital on Monday, and under the knife on Friday.

bring someone to their knees - A situation brings someone to their knees if it weakens, defeats or almosts destroys them.
The loss of its biggest contract brought the company to its knees.

A. Fill in the gaps in the sentences below with the correct Idiom from Unit 4.

1. Kids! Always wanting more and more. It's true what they say: ..give 'em an inch and they'll take a mile !

4. Wow! My luck's in today. That's three-in-a-row. Talk about ..hitting the jackpot .

2. So I'm stuck in an office and the sun is shining; I might as well .....make the best of a bad job... and get some work done.

5. Right! That's it. This has gone ..beyond a joke.. ; he's been banging away with that hammer all day. I can take no more!

3. **A:** "I've just lost 48 pounds on the bread and butter diet!"
   B: ".....No kidding..... ?"

6. "What's wrong, you say?" "Well, ..for a start......... , it took 28 days to be delivered and it was supposed to take 12."

7. **A:** "We were making fun of John the whole night, but he just laughed it off." **B:** "He must be well able to ...take a joke...."

8. Woohoo! Jackpot baby! That's three ...of a kind............. .

9. I'm so nervous! This is the first time I've ever gone ...under the knife...........; and hopefully the last!

10. I'm not sure what it was, but it was delicious - ....a kind of............... custard tart, I think.

11. That promotion the boss gave me was just like ...the kiss of death.............; I've never been more unhappy here.

12. The sight of the forest cut down and destroyed ...brought.. the poor man ..to his knees........ .

B. Choose the correct answer **A, B**, **C** or **D**.

13. Please, enough now. I've been through a lot of pain already; must you .... ?
    a. take a joke
    b. bring me to my knees
    c. make the best of a bad job
    d. give them an inch and let them take a mile

14. A: "Okay, so what did I do wrong?"
    B: "You want a list! Well, ... , you cheated on your girlfriend."
    a. for a start
    b. beyond a joke
    c. no kidding
    d. take a joke

15. Welcome to Dubai! Minus 3 degrees and counting. Wasn't this supposed to be a sun holiday? Oh well! Let's ....
    a. make the best of a bad job
    b. hit the jackpot
    c. give 'em and inch and let them take a mile
    d. bring them to their knees

16. Don't say yes to their request. Believe me, you .... ; you'll regret it, I guarantee.
    a. make the best of a bad job
    b. go under the knife
    c. give them the kiss of death
    d. give 'em an inch and they'll take a mile

17. You weren't afraid? I mean, I'd be terrified to be ....
    a. going under the knife
    b. making the best of a bad job
    c. bringing them to their knees
    d. taking a joke

18. I never want too much praise; it's ....
    a. the kiss of death
    b. taking a joke
    c. bringing me to my knees
    d. giving them an inch and then they take a mile

19. What you said was just stupid and wrong; it went ....; you should apologise.
    a. and hit the jackpot
    b. under the knife
    c. for a start
    d. beyond a joke

20. Oh, stop being so serious; your problem is you just can't ....
    a. go beyond a joke
    b. bring me to my knees
    c. hit the jackpot
    d. take a joke

21. You really .... with that gorgeous girlfriend of yours, George. She's perfect!
    a. got the kiss of death
    b. hit the jackpot
    c. went beyond a joke
    d. made the best of a bad job

22. You were in France last year! .... ? Me, too.
    a. No kidding
    b. Bring me to my knees
    c. Take a joke
    d. For a start

23. Look at those two! Like father, like son. They're ....
    a. two of a kind
    b. under the knife
    c. a kind of two
    d. taking a joke

24. It was .... disaster; I mean, from the moment we got there, we knew this holiday would be hell!
    a. no kidding
    b. a kind of
    c. brought to our knees
    d. for a start

C. Match the Definitions with the correct Idioms. There are 3 extra Idioms that do not match with any Definition.

25. For people who take advantage of your kind acts, we say...

26. To win big.

27. Make a bad situation tolerable.

28. Not funny anymore.

29. To laugh at yourself with others.

30. To begin with.

31. We're not sure exactly what it is, but it's ...... something.

32. Friends who have the same interests are two...

33. Well-intentioned, but leading to misfortune.

34. Having surgery.

35. Almost destroy a person.

36. Are you serious?

25.	e
26.	l
27.	b
28.	n
29.	o
30.	m
31.	g
32.	j
33.	a
34.	i
35.	f
36.	k

a. the kiss of death

b. make the best of a bad job

c. work your guts out

d. break new ground

e. give 'em an inch and they'll take a mile

f. bring them to their knees

g. a kind of

h. get to grips with

i. under the knife

j. of a kind

k. no kidding?

l. hit the jackpot

m. for a start

n. beyond a joke

o. take a joke

D. Fill in the gaps with the correct Idiom.

With most kids, they'll take advantage of you; **(37)** give them an inch and they'll take a mile . That's why I think we're lucky with our little Timmy. In fact, we've really **(38)** hit the jackpot . You see, Timmy is the sweetest child I've ever known. **(39)** For a start , he's not at all loud, disruptive or noisy, which is a big bonus. Then there's the fact that his personality is so well-balanced; he's intelligent, fun-loving, funny, kind, caring and considerate. I really hope I don't **(40)** give him the kiss of death by saying this, but I think our Timmy is destined for greatness. Even the doctors and nurses at the hospital said so last year when he had to go **(41)** under the knife for a minor operation. They thought he was a very special little fellow. He used to **(42)** bring them to their knees ; they were so weak from laughing at his jokes. And the nice thing about Timmy is he can be the butt of humour, too; he's well able to **(43)** take a joke .

Uhh! When I think about that little chap who lives down the road from us, I'm so grateful to have Timmy. Jack's his name, I think - the boy down the road. He's **(44)** a/some kind of little monster, let me tell you. I don't know how his parents can cope with the trouble he causes, but I guess they have to **(45)** make the best of a bad job . Jack and his evil little sister - they're two **(46)** of a kind - did something that made me rage with madness one day. Their antics went completely **(47)** beyond a joke . When I came home I found my poor little Timmy hanging on the washing line with the clothes that day, and in the pouring rain, too. There he was, wet to the bone, but still a big smile on his little face. Well, if I get hold of those two brats, they'll be sorry!

When I told Jack 's father what they'd been up to, he couldn't believe it. "**(48)** No kidding? " he said. Uhh. Some children!

E. Do the CrossWord Puzzle, finding the correct IDIOM from Unit 4.

ACROSS

5. I wouldn't call him a friend exactly; more ....a kind of............ acquaintance.

7. Now look; you've made her cry. This has gone ......beyond a joke........ .

8. You know what they say happens when you give people an inch; they .....take a mile.............. .

9. It's a bad job to be sure, but we've just got to .....make the best................... of it.

10. You don't know how to swim. ....No kidding........... ?

11. Although a draw is not a bad result, it could be ....the kiss of death..... for their hopes of winning the championship this year.

12. Typical; you can make fun of other people, but you haven't learned how to ....take a joke................ yourself now, have you?

DOWN

1. Yes! I've matched a pair; two ....of a kind.............. beats your jack-high.

2. The bank has brought me ....to my knees........... ; I can't repay the debts I owe - it's over.

3. When do you go ......under the knife.... to get that lump removed then?

4. A: "Is there some sort of problem, sir?" B: "Well, ...for a start.......... , you're standing on my foot!"

6. If we can broker this deal, we'll have ....hit the jackpot....... ; we'll be rich I tell you!

IDIOMS

in the least	**to the letter**	**tie the knot**
leave someone standing	go to great lengths	at large
let it drop	**knock it off**	**keep up with the Joneses**
let it slip	the fast lane	last but not least

in the least - You use "in the least" to emphasize a statement in the negative.
She wasn't in the least surprised to hear the news.

leave someone standing - You leave someone standing when you are much better than them at something.
Her singing left the rest of the contestants standing; they never had a chance.

let it drop - You let it drop when you stop talking about something because it is not having any effect.
But don't think I'm going to let it drop; I'll find out your reasons, one way or another.

let it slip - If you let a piece of secret information slip, you tell someone about it unintentionally.
Try not to let it slip that we're organising something for her 21st birthday; I'd really like it to be a surprise.

to the letter - You follow instructions, for example, to the letter when you follow them exactly, paying attention to every detail.
I don't understand it; I followed your guidelines to the letter, and it still doesn't work.

go to great lengths - Spend a lot of time on something, or put in a lot of effort in order to do or achieve it.
Greta Garbo went to great lengths to hide from reporters and photographers.

knock it off - You say "knock it off!" to someone if you want them to stop doing something which is annoying you.
Knock it off, will you? Some people are trying to sleep around here.

the fast lane - Someone who lives their life in the fast lane has a very busy, competitive and risky lifestyle.
His face was beginning to show the strain of life in the fast lane.

tie the knot - Get married.
We met 4 years ago, and we tied the knot last June.

at large - A dangerous person or animal that is at large has escaped from prison or captivity and has not yet been recaptured.
"You don't think that fellow Fred could have done it?" asked James. "From what I gather, he's still at large."

keep up with the Joneses - When people try to keep up with the Joneses, their competitive nature makes them try to do the same things that their neighbours or friends have done, only better.
Poorer families who see the superior goods being purchased by their rich neighbours may attempt to keep up with the Joneses and spend money they don't have.

last but not least - Last but not least is used before mentioning a person or thing that is last in a list, in order to emphasise that they are as important as those mentioned before.
Artists' statements, interviews, catalogues, biographies, chronologies, memoirs, and, last but not least, exhibition catalogues and all available this week.

A. Fill in the gaps in the sentences below with the correct Idiom from Unit 5.

1. The students weren't ....in the least....... interested in Mr. McDonald's lecture.

4. Timmy is so good at weight-lifting that he just .....leaves Mike ..standing............. .

2. Tina kept saying no to Brian's requests for a date, but he wouldn't ...let it drop.... , so eventually she agreed.

5. Whatever you do, don't ....let it slip....... to Katie that we've organised a surprise birthday party for her.

3. I don't understand; I followed these instructions ..to the letter... and I still can't piece it together.

6. Betty went ..to great lengths. to look as good as she could for her date with Dazz.

7. Oh for goodness' sake! It's three o'clock in the morning; will you ever just ....knock it off.......... ?

10. Dear me! When will people learn to slow down and relax? You can't always live life ....in the fast lane... .

8. I can't believe Mary and Alan have finally .....tied the knot..! I wonder, what took them so long?

11. Extreme care should be exercised in the area around the Zoo today; an elephant has escaped and is ...at large·· .

9. Talk about trying to ..keep up with the Joneses . They're so pathetic; we get a hot tub and they have to build a pool.

12. So, we've talked about supply factors, demand factors, and now, ...last but not least. , let's look at the role of pricing.

B. Choose the correct answer **A**, **B**, **C** or **D**.

13. Failure to follow the school rules .... will result in your immediate expulsion.
    a. to great lengths
    b. to the letter
    c. in the fast lane
    d. at large

14. Alison .... to show Rowan how much she loved him .
    a. knocked it off
    b. went to the letter
    c. let it slip
    d. went to great lengths

15. I can't believe you're engaged! When are you officially ....?
    a. in the least
    b. tying the knot
    c. letting it drop
    d. letting it slip

16. I didn't realise that Sandra was trying to keep it quiet, so I accidentally .... to John.
    a. went to great lengths
    b. let it slip
    c. tied the knot
    d. let it drop

17. Ha ha! I totally .... in that race. I was the clear winner by a mile!
    a. knocked it off
    b. let it slip
    c. was at large
    d. left you standing

18. And, ... , let me introduce our final contestant on today's show; a warm welcome for Steve everybody!
    a. last but not least
    b. at large
    c. keeping up with the Joneses
    d. to the letter

19. Reports suggest an armed convict is .... in the downtown area.
    a. in the fast lane
    b. knocking it off
    c. at large
    d. going to great lengths

20. Simon, who cares about the neighbours' new sauna? We don't have to worry about ....
    a. being at large
    b. tying the knot
    c. living life in the fast lane
    d. keeping up with the Joneses

21. So, how are you? Still going a hundred miles a minute? Living life .... ?
    a. at large
    b. in the least
    c. in the fast lane
    d. to keep up with the Joneses

22. Okay, okay. I'm going to clean the car after the match, Lisa. Stop going on about it. Will you please just .... now? I said I would.
    a. let it drop
    b. leave it standing
    c. let it slip
    d. go to great lengths

23. Be warned; I'm not afraid of you .... ; you can't bully me.
    a. in the least
    b. in the fast lane
    c. to the letter
    d. tying the knot

24. Ouch! Hey, ... Jesper! That really hurt you idiot!
    a. let it drop
    b. let it slip
    c. leave me standing
    d. knock it off

C. Match the Definitions with the correct Idiom. There are 3 extra Idioms that do not match with any Definition.

25. Emphasising the negative; not at all.

26. Perform way better than them.

27. Please stop discussing the issue; please...

28. Tell someone something by accident.

29. Follow the rules strictly; follow them...

30. With great effort.

31. Stop doing something annoying.

32. A hectic pace of life; life...

33. Get married.

34. Roaming around free, and possibly a danger to the public.

35. Competition with people near where you live to have the best things.

36. The final thing, but not the thing of the least importance.

25.	l
26.	d
27.	c
28.	n
29.	e
30.	b
31.	j
32.	m
33.	f
34.	o
35.	k
36.	g

a. make the best of a bad job

b. to great lengths

c. let it drop

d. leave them standing

e. to the letter

f. tie the knot

g. last but not least

h. take a joke

i. under the knife

j. knock it off

k. keeping up with the Joneses

l. not in the least

m. in the fast lane

n. let it slip

o. at large

D. Fill in the gaps with the correct Idiom.

A: I can't believe Mark and Jennifer are finally **(37)** ....._tying the knot_......... ; isn't it wonderful!

B: I'm not **(38)** ...._in the least_............ bit surprised. After all, it's plain for everyone to see that they're madly in love.

A: Mark went **(39)** ...._to great lengths_....... to woo her, though I wonder what took them so long to make up their minds?

B: Well, you know how Mark likes to do things **(40)** ....._to the letter_........... ; he wanted to wait until he had her father's permission before asking her to marry him.

A: Silly old-fashioned notion - asking the dad; who cares what he thinks?

B: Oh **(41)** ...._let it drop_........... , Linda; you're always going on about people being too old-fashioned. I think it was sweet.

A: Okay, okay. Sorry! Well, it's wonderful news anyway, and about time! When did they officially announce their engagement?

B: They didn't! So don't **(42)** ...._let it slip_........... to anyone yet, do you hear?

A: Me? I would never do that!

B: Yeah? What about that time last year when Tom asked you to keep my surprise party secret and you told everyone - including me!

A: Oh **(43)** ...._knock it off_......... Sarah and stop teasing me! You know I was just so excited.

B: Yeah, I know. Besides, I still managed to fool everyone into thinking I was surprised!

A: By the way, I meant to ask you; how's the new job? What's the life of an important businesswoman like these days?

B: What? You mean life **(44)** ...._in the fast lane_....... ? Yeah, the job's going well. At least now I'll finally be able to get that tennis court I've always wanted out back; that'll show the Molloys!

A: That's typical of you Linda; always trying to **(45)** _keep up with the Joneses_ . When will you learn?! You don't have to keep competing with everyone. You **(46)** ..._left_....... most of us poor ordinary folk ...._standing_............... years ago!

B: Oh it's not like that. I just want to wipe the smile off that smug Mr Molloy's face!

A: Whatever you say! Oh and **(47)** ......_last_........ but most certainly not ..._least_..... , I meant to ask you; will I see you tonight?

B: Is it safe?

A: What do you mean?

B: Well, isn't that escaped murderer still supposed to be **(48)** ......_at large_................. ?

A: Oh don't be silly; he's probably miles away by now.

E. Do the CrossWord Puzzle, finding the correct IDIOM from Unit 5.

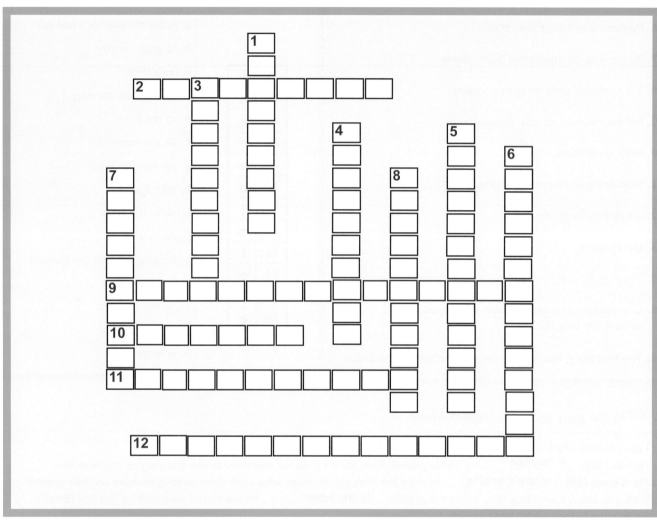

ACROSS

2. If she's not going to listen to you, then why don't you just ......let it drop........... .

9. And now, ...last but not least...... , let me introduce my co-star, Cheryl Crawley.

10. He has been ....at large........... for six weeks; you'd think the police would have found him by now.

11. Eventually, life in ....the fast lane....... is going to take its toll on you.

12. Stop trying to keep up ......with the Joneses..... ; focus on making your family happy instead.

DOWN

1. Whatever you do, don't ....let it slip............... to anyone; this is supposed to be our secret.

3. So, come on, tell me; when are you two going to finally ....tie the knot...... ?

4. Don't you two ever get tired of arguing with each other? Why don't you ...knock it off.............. ?

5. And that is how it should be done; ....leave........ your opponents ....standing........ in your wake!

6. Thank you for going ....to... such ....great lengths........ to find this book for me Roger - you shouldn't have!

7. A: "Aren't you interested in this lecture?" B: "Not ....in the least............. ."

8. We have to apply the law ....to the letter......... , otherwise we could be accused of favouritism.

Revision Test 1

Units 1-5

A. Match the first half of the sentence with the second half containing the correct Idiom.

1. We're getting reports from the Dublin area that an elephant has escaped from Fossetts' Circus and is

2. He lost all his wealth in a weekend of gambling-madness, which just goes to show that

3. I can't speak very clearly; I have

4. You're letting the kids do whatever they want; you need to

5. I'm glad we're getting along well; I hate that we

6. You might not like the situation, but you'll just have to

7. How could you say that? It's not funny; this is

8. I'm not sure exactly what it was, but it tasted like a

9. You two are quite the pair; yes, very definitely two

10. You might think you are helping, but trust me, with that kind of advice, you might as well just give her

11. I have to say well done; this time, you beat me

12. You don't want to be seen eating alone in public, do you? I think you're afraid of

13. I'm flying to New York this morning and then on to London this afternoon; talk about life

14. You must follow the rules of this competition

15. Why do you want to destroy me? You are determined to

16. I hear the operation's tomorrow. You must be nervous going

17. Oh I was only kidding; lighten up! You just aren't able to

18. He has been in this business a long time. Sure now he's

19. You could never have managed on your own; lucky I was

20. You mean you've never been to London,

1.	g
2.	k
3.	a
4.	b
5.	e
6.	o
7.	s
8.	t
9.	f
10.	q
11.	d
12.	i
13.	n
14.	l
15.	h
16.	r
17.	j
18.	c
19.	m
20.	p

a. a frog in my throat.

b. put your foot down.

c. an old hand.

d. fair and square.

e. got off on the wrong foot.

f. of a kind.

g. at large.

h. bring me to my knees.

i. losing face.

j. take a joke.

k. a fool and his money are soon parted.

l. to the letter.

m. on hand!

n. in the fast lane!

o. grin and bear it.

p. no kidding?

q. the kiss of death.

r. under the knife.

s. beyond a joke.

t. kind of chocolate cake.

B. Write **C** or **I** (**Correct** or **Incorrect**) in the boxes, for each sentence, using an Idiom.

21. I'm so pleased I gave them the day off; give 'em an inch and they'll take a mile, you see.	**21.** I
22. Maybe it's pouring with rain, but let's not be sad; it's time to make the best of a bad job.	**22.** C
23. Why do I dislike him? Well, for a start, he's an arrogant man.	**23.** C
24. 'Although he hit the jackpot, it didn't move, so he lost.	**24.** I
25. I hear you have been holding the fort in the shop while Alice is on sick leave - and doing quite well, rumour has it!	**25.** C
26. The successful suit of the tobacco firm opened the floodgates to more new claims.	**26.** C
27. To have received the *Employee of the Month* award is certainly a feather in your cap.	**27.** C
28. That figures about £225, or am I adding it up wrong?	**28.** I
29. You can't work your fingers to the bone day in, day out; it's unhealthy.	**29.** C
30. I worked my guts out all over the floor.	**30.** I
31. I don't think you should get it shaved; keep your hair on.	**31.** I
32. I bet you haven't got the guts to ask her out!	**32.** C
33. If this experiment we're doing is a success, we will be breaking new ground.	**33.** C
34. Look at those two - hand in glove - they make a great team.	**34.** C
35. It was a very close match and they won hands down.	**35.** I
36. I gave him a free hand to do what he likes, but he'd better make it a success.	**36.** C
37. What a display by the Korean archer! He left the rest of the field standing.	**37.** C
38. It's time to let it drop Tom, she's not going to change her mind.	**38.** C
39. Knock it off you two; that racket is driving me crazy!	**39.** C
40. They tried to keep up with the Joneses, but the Joneses crossed the finished line a yard ahead.	**40.** I

C. Fill in the gaps in the text with the correct form of the Idioms from the box below.

in the least	take your fancy	hold your ground	(not) let the grass grow under your feet
let it slip	drag your feet	give as good as you get	
tie the knot	get cold feet	up to no good	
to great lengths	fingers crossed	make the grade	
last but not least	have your hands full	flash in the pan	the grass is always greener on the other side
save face	get to grips with	fools rush in	

I wasn't (41).......in the least........ impressed by Glen when we first met. To be honest, he didn't really (42)...........take my fancy... at all. You see, I don't normally find guys who are big and strong with lots of muscles attractive, so it definitely wasn't a case of love at first sight. But Glen went (43).....to great lengths.......... to get my attention and his persistence paid off. And once I got to know him better, I started to really like him. After a while it became clear that our romance was a serious one; it was no (44).......flash in the pan........ affair. What I liked most about Glen was his honesty and humility. Glen was never interested in trying to (45)...................save face.................... ; when he made a mistake, he'd just come out and admit it - and apologise in front of a whole room of people if necessary; he wouldn't care. Another thing that impressed me was his attitude. He was always busy, always moving forward and working hard. Glen was never one to (46)....let the grass grow under his feet...... . And, (47).........last but not least...... , there was his charm and kindness. Glen has a beautiful heart and a lovely way with people. My one fault with him is that he is a bit of a mischief-maker; he's always (48).......up to no good........... - but in a good-natured way, of course. I suppose he's a bit of a practical joker. But, let me tell you, I can (49).give as good as I get....... ! I know a joke or two as well!

I've always been happy with what I've got. I've never been one to believe (50)..the grass is always greener on the other side... . It's green enough where I am already! But one thing did worry me; Glen seemed to be (51).....dragging his feet........ about asking me to marry him. Of course, it's true, only (52)..........fools rush in........ , but I wasn't in a hurry - the fact is we had been going out together for four years. I was worried that he might be (53) ...getting cold feet . Was he afraid of commitment? Then one day he accidentally (54)................let it slip.......... . It wasn't a proposal really; he just started talking about marriage before he'd had a chance to think about what he was saying - and now we're officially engaged! I'm over the moon! We (55)......tie the knot............ in April next year. (56).........Fingers crossed........ , everything will go really well. I certainly hope so. Of course, before we could plan the wedding, there was one big problem to deal with - my father. No man was ever good enough for my father. No man had ever (57)........made the grade....... . I was hoping Glen would be the first to learn to deal with him, but my father was difficult to (58).......get to grips with..... . Glen handled himself really well though and confidently (59).....held his ground........ . "Mr Long", he said, "I love your daughter and I want to marry her, and I am not afraid of you even though you try to scare all the men in your daughter's life away. But I would like your blessing. She is my world and I will treat her like a princess; that, I promise." To which my father replied: "Ha! Princess! Poor fellow! You're going to (60)...have your hands full.... with her young man. She's a lot of hard work! But best of luck to you lad." - And that was my father's way of telling us we were getting married!

	IDIOMS	
larger than life	**the bottom line**	**at a loss**
true to life	be/step out of line	tough/hard luck
cast (some) light on something	**a load of rubbish**	**push your luck**
in light of	use your loaf	to the best of your knowledge

larger than life - someone who has a strong, vibrant personality, and always appears to be full of energy and enthusiasm; something that is larger than life makes a very strong impression on you.
She was larger than life; she was game for anything; she was jolly and vibrant, and spoke her mind; all in all, she was fun to be with.

true to life - Something such as a painting or story that is described as true to life closely resembles reality.
These portraits appear reassuringly true to life and easy to understand.

cast (some) light on something - Someone or something that casts light on a situation provides information which makes it easier to understand.
Are there any elements in your upbringing which might help to explain or cast light on who you are, and how you behave and respond?

in light of - You make a decision in light of a particular fact, when you base your decision on that knowledge.
In the light of what we have just heard about the pending corruption charges, I think it would be wise to reassess our decision to invest in Bangs Incorporated.

the bottom line - The final result, the most basic fact, or the most important consideration of a situation, activity or discussion.
Okay, enough of all this talk; what's the bottom line?

be/step out of line - start behaving in a way that is wrong or inappropriate, or that is not allowed or expected of you.
How dare you question my authority? You are way out of line young man.

a load of rubbish - Something that is worthless, untrue or nonsensical.
The pop star described reports of a breakdown in her marriage as a load of rubbish, indicating that she was very happy and content in her personal affairs.

use your loaf - To use your loaf is to use your intelligence or think carefully about something.
What do you mean 'why is she upset?' Oh, for heaven's sake, use your loaf; she just broke up with her boyfriend of eight years.

at a loss - You are at a loss when you are puzzled or shocked and do not know what to do or say.
You are going to give every last penny of your fortune to charity? I'm at a loss for words.

tough luck or **hard luck** - You say "tough luck" or "hard luck" to someone when something unfortunate has happened to them, either to show sympathy, or ironically, as a way of saying that the person will have to accept the situation.
A: "We lost."   B: "Ah, that's too bad. Hard luck."

push your luck - Someone is pushing their luck, if they are risking disappointment or failure, or might cause trouble by trying to gain too much, or by asking for too much or being too demanding.
It's almost 2:30. You're pushing your luck if you think you can make it to the airport in time for your flight - you'd better hurry.

to the best of your knowledge - You say that something is true to the best of your knowledge if you think it is true based on what you know, but you aren't completely sure.
The information was, to the best of my knowledge, accurate when I made the speech a week ago. All our intelligence data indicated that they did have weapons of mass destruction.

A. Fill in the gaps in the sentences below with the correct Idiom from Unit 6.

1. Mary had a ...larger than life..... personality. The interviewers loved her and she got the job.

2. **A:** "Are you finished already? I still have eight more questions to do; I'll be up all night." **B:** "....Tough luck... I guess!"

3. Oh, will you all just stop talking such ...a load of rubbish... ! All I want to know is what the bottom line is.

4. **A:** "That book was very true to life." **B:** "I agree. And it ...cast light on... the darker side of the human mind."

5. You know Tim, to the best of my knowledge, no one has ever successfully carried out an experiment like this before.

6. "....In light of... the fact that you have been littering the streets, I hereby fine you £100", said the judge to Alice.

7. The bottom line... is that, no matter what these reports say, my business is profitable and successful; people should invest.

8. He tried hard to think of a good present, but Timothy was ...at a loss... for what to buy Mary for her birthday.

9. Paul knew he had ..pushed his luck.. too far by trying to back-heel the ball into the net; his miss cost the team the game.

10. For once, Mark had made up his mind to solve his problems logically; he decided to ...use his loaf... .

11. The film is very .....true to life... ; the hero is someone who loses more often than he wins; and don't we all!

12. What a great employee; she never ever ..steps out of line. She just gets on with her work quietly, doing her best.

B. Choose the correct answer **A, B**, **C** or **D**.

13. Look at the way the artist has depicted the sadness in the boy's face; that's ....
    a. tough luck
    b. stepping out of line
    c. very true to life
    d. pushing your luck

14. Know this: if you .... once more, you will be fired on the spot. Do you understand?
    a. are at a loss
    b. use your loaf
    c. step out of line
    d. cast light on it

15. .... your confession, I hereby place you under arrest. You have the right to remain silent.
    a. The bottom line of
    b. In light of
    c. Cast light on
    d. Step out of line with

16. That fellow is really .... He's worked here for less than two weeks and he's already asking for a raise.
    a. at a loss
    b. pushing his luck
    c. a load of rubbish
    d. true to life

17. Great shot! .... though; it just missed the line by a few inches.
    a. Hard luck
    b. Use your loaf
    c. Larger than life
    d. True to life

18. A: "Why is Brad looking so upset?"
    B: "Oh, why don't you .... ? He has just lost the love of his life - how would you feel in his position?
    a. use your loaf
    b. cast light on it
    c. push your luck
    d. step out of line

19. She certainly made an impression on him! I've never seen him .... for words like that before.
    a. use his loaf
    b. larger than life
    c. at a loss
    d. cast light on it

20. .... he plays centre-back for Chelsea, but I can't be sure.
    a. Cast light on the fact that
    b. Tough luck that
    c. To the best of my knowledge
    d. Use your loaf

21. Those rumours are .... I've met Mel and she is a lovely, kind-hearted woman.
    a. true to life
    b. a load of rubbish
    c. to the best of my knowledge
    d. pushing your luck

22. Can you .... what's happening in this film? Because I haven't got any idea.
    a. push your luck over
    b. step out of line with
    c. use your loaf about
    d. cast some light on

23. I have heard all your excuses before. Just tell me, what's .... ? Will we make a profit this year?
    a. a load of rubbish
    b. the bottom line
    c. larger than life
    d. to the best of your knowledge

24. A: "Goodness, that Bill's a character, isn't he?"
    B: ".............. ! Penny will have her hands full with him I think!"
    a. To the best of his knowledge
    b. Larger than life
    c. True to life
    d. Don't push your luck

C. Match the Definitions with the correct Idiom. There are 3 extra Idioms that do not match with any Definition.

25. Full of energy and character.

26. Very like reality.

27. Help to explain.

28. Based on (some information).

29. Apply your intelligence.

30. Nonsense.

31. Not knowing what to do.

32. That's unfortunate!

33. Risk too much.

34. Considering everything I know.

35. What are the simple facts? What is ..... ?

36. Behave in a way that you shouldn't.

25.	k
26.	c
27.	j
28.	l
29.	o
30.	n
31.	m
32.	f
33.	a
34.	b
35.	h
36.	g

a. push your luck

b. to the best of my knowledge

c. true to life

d. by all means

e. make your mark

f. tough luck

g. step out of line

h. the bottom line

i. quick off the mark

j. cast some light on

k. larger than life

l. in light of

m. at a loss

n. a load of rubbish

o. use your loaf

D. Fill in the gaps with the correct Idiom.

My brother Bill has always loved attention. He has a big personality and the energy of 20 people. Everyone who meets him says that he is **(37)** larger than life . **(38)** To the best of my knowledge .. though, he has never ever upset anyone and there isn't a bad bone in his body. Truth be told, I'm amazed he is so optimistic. After all, he has had his fair share of **(39)** hard luck in life. When his wife passed away, we were **(40)** at a loss for what to do. But Bill, as ever, was resilient and he put a brave face on, even though he was crying inside. A year after her passing, and life is finally getting back to normal for him.

The kids have kept him going he says. Tina, his youngest, is a lovely girl. But she's very demanding, and she is always **(41)** pushing her luck - some day she'll be sorry she does that as she risks Bill losing his patience and getting angry with her. His eldest, Rob, takes after him. He's always talking **(42)** a load of rubbish , but he is a real character, too, and, just like his father, everybody loves him! Rob is a great help to his dad. **(43)** The bottom line is without Rob I don't think Bill would have survived. He keeps his spirits up.

Last Saturday, Bill and I had lunch for the first time in ages. He looked well. Afterwards, he took me to see some big new release. I thought it was pretty awful, but Bill really liked it. He said it was **(44)** true to life ; how people really feel. Then I thought about it afterwards and realised the lead character and Bill had a lot in common. They had both been through the pain of the loss of a loved one. I had never expected Bill to like such a deep movie, though. His comments about it **(45)** cast light on his real feelings and helped me understand how much pain he must have felt when Laura died.

We had a really great day together and, **(46)** in light of that, we're going to make our Saturday get-together a regular thing. The only problem is that Bill says he's going to bring Tina along with him next time. Well, she'd better not **(47)** step out of line though because I don't have as much patience as Bill! If she does anything wrong, she'll be sorry. Sometimes Tina comes out with some really stupid things. I wish she'd **(48)** use her loaf a bit more instead of using her mouth so much. There won't be a minute's peace next Saturday while she's around!

E. Do the CrossWord Puzzle, finding the correct IDIOM from Unit 6.

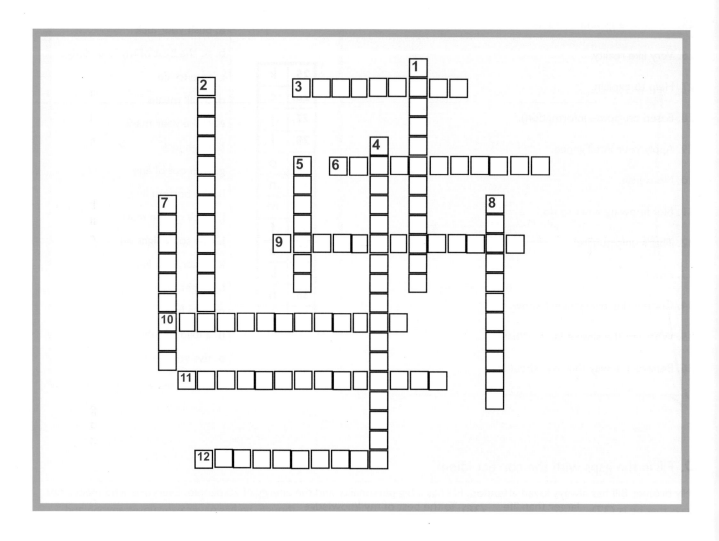

ACROSS

3. If you don't want to do it, ...tough luck........... ; I'm not giving you any choice in the matter.

6. Oh, will you ....use your loaf.......... for once Paul - or do I have to show you how to do everything?

9. Do you ever get tired of talking such a ....load of rubbish.......... ? Because I know I get tired of hearing it!

10. If you want me to remain working for your company, you'll have to pay me more money; that's ....the bottom line.......... .

11. Sheena is ....larger than life.......... . She has the biggest, most outrageous personality of anyone I've ever met.

12. I have to compliment the script writer for keeping the storyline so ....true to life.......... .

DOWN

1. You really decided to ....push your luck.......... a bit didn't you? Don't you think it's a bit dangerous to attempt a climb to the summit without any oxygen tanks to have, at least on standby, for emergencies?

2. I don't want to ....step out of line.......... , but someone has to tell you what you did is wrong.

4. To the very ....best of my knowledge.......... , he moved down south about a year ago.

5. She was ....at a loss.......... to explain how the chocolate bar had found its way from the shelf into her handbag.

7. ....In light of.......... all the evidence put before me today, I find the defendant guilty as charged.

8. Would either of you care to ......cast...... some ......light on.......... what is going on?

IDIOMS

make your mark	**a means to an end**	**make it up**
quick off the mark	within your means	in the making
beyond your means	**make do**	**lose your marbles**
by all means	make it	leave your/a mark

make your mark - to first become successful or influential in a particular field, or to make a very significant contribution to something that is widely recognised.
What a performance this young player is putting in today! He is determined to make his mark.

quick off the mark - You are quick off the mark if your mind works quickly or you have quick reactions in a situation.
Michael was very good at improvising; he was very bright and quick off the mark.

beyond your means - A person is living beyond their means when they spend more money than they earn, or than they can afford to.
Credit cards just encourage people to live beyond their means.

by all means - You say "by all means" as a polite way of giving permission for someone to do something; you can also use it as a polite way of saying 'yes' or 'of course'.
A: "Excuse me. Could you take a photograph of my girlfriend and I in front of the statue?" B: "By all means."

a means to an end - something that you do not do for enjoyment but rather to achieve something, or to fulfil a specific purpose or goal; it is something that you do to help you to get something else that you want more.
This internship is a means to an end. Once I am fully trained, I plan on applying for the role of team leader.

within your means - A price to be paid for something is within your means if you have enough money to afford it or buy it; someone is living within their means if they do not spend more money that they earn or have.
It's hard to live within your means when the only money you have coming in is Income Support.

make do - You make do, or make do with something, when you accept it or make the best use of it, even though it is not exactly what you wanted, because nothing better is available to you.
If we can't get butter, we'll just have to make do with margarine.

make it - You make it when you are successful in doing or being something.
I never hear from him any more now that he's made it as a pop singer.

make it up - You make it up to someone you have disappointed when you do something for them as a way of apologising; or when you do something that makes them feel better after you originally did something bad to them.
A: "I've been waiting for hours. Where are you?"
B: "Sorry love. I'm stuck in a business meeting; I don't think I will be able to go to dinner tonight. I'll make it up to you at the weekend, I promise."

in the making - "In the making" describes a person or thing that is developing into something.
Here is a talented musician in the making.

lose your marbles - If you say that someone is losing their marbles, you mean that they are going mad, or becoming forgetful and confused.
A: "Granny, why are you setting the table again? We've only just had dinner?"
B: "Sorry dear, your poor granny must be losing her marbles!"

leave your/a mark - To leave a/your mark on someone or something is to have a strong and noticeable effect on them, often a bad one that lasts for a long time.
Years of conflict have left a mark on this once beautiful country.

Illustrated English Idioms

A. Fill in the gaps in the sentences below with the correct Idiom from Unit 7.

1. David's work at the publishing house was only a means to an end. All he really wanted was to get his own poetry published.

4. A: "Mark, will you show me that new exercise routine you used to lose all that weight?" **B:** "By all means. ."

2. I'll never ......make it... up the stairs carrying this on my own; I'm about to collapse!

5. Frank refused the offer of financial assistance from his neighbour Ron. He was determined to live within his means.

3. Miss Gainor was very quick off the mark.. . She knew Sam was up to no good and warned him to stop misbehaving.

6. Her problem is she doesn't know when to stop; she just carries on using credit cards and spending .beyond her means.

7. The chef had run out of butter, so he had to ....make do....... with margarine for his 'special' cake recipe.

10. This kid is a phenomenon! He's definitely a pop star in the making ....

8. To make it up to Sue for not being able to go on the vacation they'd planned for her birthday, he met her at the airport.

11. Nobody has heard of 'Boogie Nights' yet, but they are determined to make their mark and become big popstars.

9. If I get asked just one more question by the press I think I am going to lose my marbles... . This is driving me mad!

12. Bob Marley really ....left his mark... on the world of music; he created a new type called reggae, after all.

B. Choose the correct answer **A, B**, **C** or **D**.

13. I'm surprised she hasn't .... with ten children to look after. How does she cope?
    a. made do
    b. made it
    c. made her mark
    d. lost all her marbles

14. Look at that posture - brilliant! Now there's a ballerina .... if ever I saw one.
    a. losing her marbles
    b. making it up
    c. in the making
    d. within her means

15. You'd better .... ; that's the third time you've cancelled our date this week.
    a. leave your mark
    b. make it up to me
    c. be quick off the mark
    d. make your mark

16. I know you don't want to be a receptionist all your life, but maybe with the contacts you make it can be ....
    a. a means to an end
    b. quick off the mark
    c. by all means
    d. beyond your means

17. If you want .... in this business, you have to work very hard; then success will come.
    a. to make your mark
    b. to make it up
    c. to go beyond your means
    d. to make do

18. You'll have to be .... if you want to get those cheap flights to Paris; they'll sell out fast.
    a. a means to an end
    b. quick off the mark
    c. in the making
    d. making your mark

19. .... try yourself if you don't believe me; it's impossible to do.
    a. Within your means
    b. Beyond your means
    c. Make your mark and
    d. By all means

20. That's what you get for living .... ; an unpaid credit card bill for £20,000.
    a. beyond your means
    b. within your means
    c. in the making
    d. by all means

21. It's not perfect, but it's too late to go to the shops for something different so we'll have to ....
    a. make do
    b. be quick off the mark
    c. leave a mark
    d. make it up

22. My dream is to be a famous writer, but, you know, it's a tough industry and I'm not sure if I'll be able to ....
    a. make it
    b. lose my marbles
    c. make it up
    d. be quick off the mark

23. It was wonderful to get a pay rise at work. Now we can realistically live ....
    a. within our means
    b. in the making
    c. by all means
    d. quick off the mark

24. **A:** "Oh it's terrible what has happened in Zimbabwe, isn't it?"
    B: "Why? What happened?"
    A: "Didn't you hear? Civil war has broken out. It's a disaster likely to .... on the country for a very long time to come."
    a. leave a mark
    b. make it
    c. lose its marbles
    d. be a means to an end

C. Match the Definitions with the correct Idiom. There are 3 extra Idioms that do not match with any Definition.

25. Be successful and influential, and make an important contribution.

26. Able to think on your feet; fast to react.

27. Spending more than you should is living...

28. Yes, of course.

29. A way of getting what you want eventually.

30. Become a success.

31. Use or accept what you have even though it's not perfect.

32. Not spending more money than you can afford to is living...

33. Do something special in order to apologise.

34. Have a significant and long-lasting effect.

35. Start to go crazy.

36. In the process of becoming something.

25.	c
26.	i
27.	e
28.	b
29.	a
30.	m
31.	j
32.	f
33.	l
34.	g
35.	o
36.	d

a. a means to an end

b. by all means

c. make your mark

d. in the making

e. beyond your means

f. within your means

g. leave a mark

h. push your luck

i. quick off the mark

j. make do

k. cast light on something

l. make it up

m. make it

n. tough luck

o. lose your marbles

D. Fill in the gaps with the correct Idiom.

I always give my students the same advice when they graduate; if you want to **(37)**...........make it................. in the business world, you have to work your guts out. There's no hidden secret to success. And, as business graduates, I tell them, there are certain mistakes they should never make. The most fundamental thing to remember is not to overspend; living **(38)**...within your means. is so important. If you are in debt, it will lead to stress and unhappiness in the long run. My students know it is just stupid to spend **(39)** beyond your/ their means , so they have no excuses for making this mistake when they enter the big bad world.

I have to say, I am very impressed with some of this year's graduates; they have great potential. I think there is many a millionaire **(40)**......in the making......... amongst this lot. One, in particular, has already **(41)**......made........... his mark . He set up a new online bank-comparison site and hit the jackpot. He earns more money than I do and he's barely half my age! - Never mind! I **(42)**....make do.......... with what I have. I would **(43)**....lose my marbles..... if I started comparing myself with some of my ex-students; they have so much money that I can't bear thinking about it.

Over the years, I've learned that an important factor in business start-up success is learning to be **(44)**..quick off the mark... . You have to spot the opportunity before anyone else does. And, **(45)**......by all means........... , take a gamble - but not with your own money. I've warned my students that they should never set up a business by committing their own assets because then, if it fails, they are ruined. Always seek outside investment, that's what I say! Besides, if you go bankrupt, that will **(46)**.........leave a mark......... on your character for a very long time and be hard to recover from.

Of course, not all of them will be super rich. But then, there's no shame in taking a middle-management job to begin with. That can be **(47)**.a means to an end... , and by building up experience, you can become very successful later on yourself.

In the end, it's all about finding the right balance in your work life; one that makes you happy. And if there's one other piece of advice I'd give my students before they leave, it is this; if you work very hard early on in your career, for goodness' sake **(48)**.make it up..... to your family later - they deserve your attention, too.

E. Do the CrossWord Puzzle, finding the correct IDIOM from Unit 7.

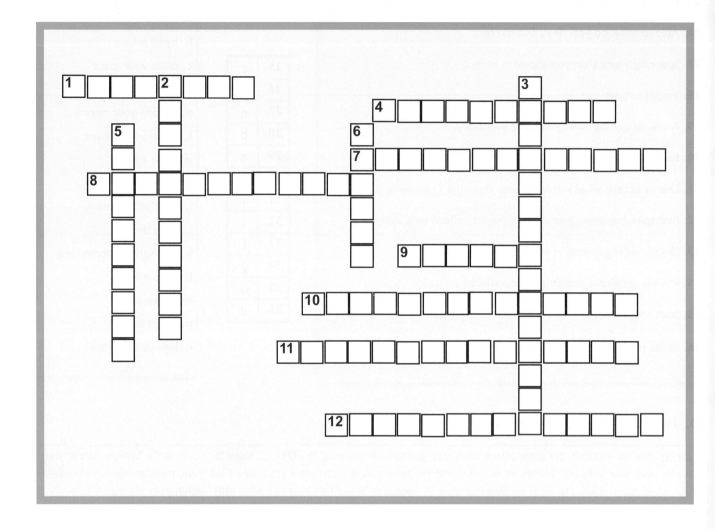

ACROSS

1. Could you work tonight's late shift for me? I'll ....make it up........ to you, I promise.

4. ....By all means...... , if she asks you out on a date say yes. After all, we've been split up for over a year now.

7. Is this just a means to an end..... , or is it what you want to do for the rest of your life?

8. You really ..made your mark..... with that performance in the second half - fantastic young man!

9. We will have to ....make do............ with three players until Paul arrives; he shouldn't be long.

10. I think Paddy has really ...lost his marbles...... ; did you see what he did in class this morning?

11. You were pretty .quick off the mark... to marry her; you've only known each other for six weeks.

12. It's not .....within his means.. to pay £300,000 for a house; that's why he asked his parents for the money.

DOWN

2. With a cast which includes Brad Pitt and Angelina Jolie, this is a blockbuster .....in the making........ .

3. The problem when you live ..beyond your means. is that eventually your debts catch up with you.

5. Famine can .....leave...a.... terrible .....mark.... on the minds of the survivors.

6. This is not a silly notion father; I really want to ....make it............ as a clown. I've enrolled in clown college and I'm going to become the best clown ever.

UNIT 8

IDIOMS

meet someone halfway	stand out a mile	money is no object
not to mention	cry over spilt milk	money talks
the more the merrier	put your money where your mouth is	in the nick of time
run a mile	have money to burn	make the most of something

meet someone halfway - You meet someone halfway if you make a compromise with them; if you refuse to do exactly what they want, but agree to change some of your plans or demands to fit in with theirs.
We'll never find a solution unless the unions are willing to meet us halfway.

not to mention - People say "not to mention" before they add a comment to emphasise what they have already said.
They've got everything in that house; fitted walk-in wardrobes, new carpets, not to mention a steam room and sauna.

the more the merrier - If someone says "the more the merrier", they mean that the more people or things there are, the better.
A: "Have you got room in the car for us?"
B: "Pile in. The more the merrier."

run a mile - You say that a certain situation would make someone run a mile if you think that person would be afraid of it, and try to escape from it.
Oh, I think she really likes me, but she'd run a mile if I mentioned marriage so soon after we started going out.

stand out a mile - You say that someone or something stands out a mile if you think they are very obvious, unusual or noticeable.
Oh, come on. You can tell how posh he is from his accent; it stands out a mile.

cry over spilt milk - to be regretful over or upset about something which you cannot change even if you want to.
So you failed the test. Big deal! There's no point in crying over spilt milk now, is there? Work hard and you'll pass the next time.

put your money where your mouth is - If you say that a person or organisation should put their money where their mouth is, you are telling them to supply money for a purpose which they claim to support.
If you are so sure Manchester United will win the derby game against Liverpool, why don't you put your money where your mouth is? I bet you ten pounds Liverpool will be victorious.

have money to burn - You say that someone has money to burn if they have enough money to be able to spend it in ways that you think are foolish; or if they simply have a huge amount of money at their disposal.
Unless you've got money to burn these expensive guitars are probably not the instruments to get you started.

money is no object - If you say that money is no object, you mean that you do not consider money to be important in the decision which you are about to make, as you can afford to spend whatever amount is necessary to obtain or achieve what you want.
She flitted from country to country as if money was no object, which, knowing Lori, probably wasn't.

money talks - If someone says "money talks", they mean that people are more likely to be persuaded to do something if you can offer them money to do it.
A spokesperson for Real Madrid was quoted as saying: "Money talks, let me assure you of that! If we make them a good enough offer, they won't be able to refuse. Rolando will be a Real Madrid player by the end of the year."

in the nick of time - You do something in the nick of time when you only just manage to do it before it is too late.
Mark escaped from the house fire in the nick of time; only ten seconds later the gas mains exploded, flattening the building.

make the most of something - You make the most of something such as an advantageous position when you use it to get as much benefit or pleasure as possible from the situation.
Make the most of your holidays when you are a student because you'll never have so much free time again.

Illustrated English Idioms

A. Fill in the gaps in the sentences below with the correct Idiom from unit 8.

1. We're never going to reach a compromise unless you agree to ...meet me halfway..... . What do you say Bianca?

4. As you can see, this house has its own garage, ...not to mention brand new double-glazing windows.

2. Why don't you join us Martina? After all, you know what they say: ...the more the merrier .

5. Sally's afraid of commitment; she'd .run.a.mile. if I proposed to her; and she'd never be seen again!

3. I'm just sort of self-conscious at the moment. Being pregnant, I feel like I ....stand out a mile..... .

6. I know you're upset the car's damaged, but what's done is done; it's no use ...crying over spilt milk .

52

7. If the minister thinks we should donate more money to charity, then why doesn't he put his money where his mouth is ?

10. Rumour has it they are mega rich! Patty told me they have money to burn . And I believe her; have you seen their car?

8. You might think money talks , but I won't be bribed into doing what you ask for any sum of money, Mister.

11. Money is no object ; he is rumoured to be one of the wealthiest men in Britain; he can have anything he wants.

9. Dave arrived just in the nick of time; ten seconds later and the door would have been bolted shut for the night.

12. Woohoo! It's the holidays and the sun is shining; let's make the most of the good weather while it lasts.

B. Choose the correct answer **A, B**, **C** or **D**.

13. I will pay whatever you ask; I want this car.
Believe me, ...
a. money is no object
b. money talks
c. you have money to burn
d. you stand out a mile

14. Thank goodness you made it - and just .... ,
too. Our reservation was about to be cancelled.
a. meet me halfway
b. in the nick of time
c. make the most of it
d. run a mile

15. Do you think we .... or something? We
don't invest in business for fun; we invest to
profit.
a. have money to burn
b. will meet you halfway
c. stand out a mile
d. put our money where our mouth is

16. Okay, so the hotel isn't as nice as we'd
expected, but at least it's got a swimming pool;
let's ....
a. make the most of it
b. cry over spilt milk
c. have money to burn
d. run a mile

17. How much will you give me to do it?
Come on; you know ....
a. stand out a mile
b. money talks
c. don't cry over spilt milk
d. run a mile

18. **A:** "I can't afford to pay that amount. I'm sorry.
£25 is too much - how about £20."
B: "Why don't you .... ?
Let's say £22.50"
A: "Okay, you have a deal. Pleasure doing
business with you!"
a. stand out a mile
b. put your money where your mouth is
c. make the most of it
d. meet me halfway

19. Look, I forgive you; I'm not going to start
.... now, am I?
a.. in the nick of time
b. having money to burn
c. crying over spilt milk
d. meeting you halfway

20. I am disappointed, ... upset, about what
you have done. It was very wrong.
a. crying over spilt milk and
b. more the merrier and
c. meeting you halfway and
d. not to mention

21. You are .... if you see Jenny today, I can tell.
You know, you can't avoid her forever though!
a. not to mention
b. in the nick of time
c. making the most of it
d. going to run a mile

22. At this party, it's a case of .... ; we've
invited half the town to come along already!
a. the more the merrier
b. in the nick of time
c. put your money where your mouth is
d. meeting them halfway

23. .... Ian. I bet you £500 they will lose the
game tomorrow. Bet with me if you're so sure!
a. Put your money where your mouth is
b. Meet me halfway
c. The more the merrier
d. Not to mention

24. I feel uncomfortable driving around in this
convertible. Don't you think .... ?
a. the more the merrier
b. money talks
c. we stand out a mile
d. we have money to burn

C. Match the Definitions with the correct Idiom. There are 3 extra Idioms that do not match with any Definition.

25. Make a compromise with them.

26. Be in possession of great wealth..

27. If you will pay anything to get what you want, then...

28. Emphasising the next point.

29. Everyone is welcome.

30. Avoid out of fear.

31. Be very noticeable.

32. Get upset over something you can't do anything about.

33. Show me that you believe what you say.

34. Just before it was too late.

35. Be happy with the situation you are in and try to enjoy it.

36. People are influenced by money.

25.	g
26.	m
27.	a
28.	i
29.	o
30.	k
31.	j
32.	n
33.	h
34.	c
35.	d
36.	e

a. money is no object

b. the bottom line

c. in the nick of time

d. make the most of it

e. money talks

f. at a loss

g. meet them halfway

h. put your money where your mouth is

i. not to mention

j. stand out a mile

k. run a mile

l. in light of

m. have money to burn

n. cry over spilt milk

o. the more the merrier

D. Fill in the gaps with the correct Idiom.

If he is prepared to (37) **meet me halfway** , then I'll make the deal - but I can't be expected to give it to him for next-to-nothing either. It's fine being generous to people, but the reality is (38) **money talks** , and I need to make a profit in order to pay the bills and keep a roof over my head, (39) **not to mention** look after my children.

In fact, if this deal does go through, it will just be (40) **in the nick of time** because my mortgage payments are in arrears; I haven't made any for two months now. I don't (41) **have money to burn** , you see; business hasn't been going well lately. There was a time a few years ago when (42) **money was no object** and I could have whatever I wanted, but those days are long gone now. But there's no point in (43) **crying over spilt milk** ; I just have to get on with life and try to (44) **make the most of it** .

I'll always regret that bad investment I made a year ago though. It nearly ruined me. The next time I see someone selling foreign rental properties, I will (45) **run a mile** . What I learned from the salesman who conned me is to ask the question; if it really is as good as they say, then why don't they (46) **put their money where their mouth is** themselves?

On the positive side, my wife Jen is organising a party for my birthday this weekend. She wants to keep it small, but (47) **the more the merrier** if you ask me - I like a big crowd. The exterior of the house is going to be covered with fairy lights - it's going to (48) **stand out a mile** , but who cares!

E. Do the CrossWord Puzzle, finding the correct IDIOM from Unit 8.

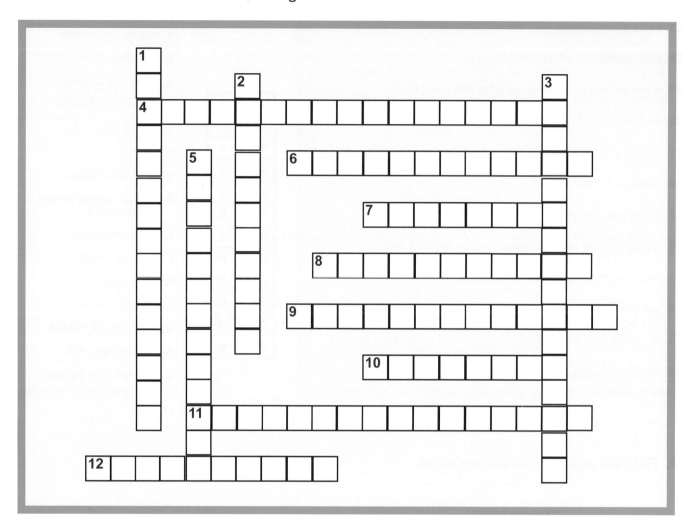

ACROSS

4. A: "Are you saying you want to do more work?" **B:** "Why not? ....The more the merrier........ ; I enjoy it!"

6. I have a lot to do to get ready for tomorrow's party, ...not to mention................ the family get-together the night after.

7. If he asks you for money, ...run a mile............. . That would be my advice.

8. Well, although my life hasn't been perfect, at least I've ....made the most.......... of it!

9. I ....stood out a mile........ in Africa; I'm fair-skinned and a redhead you see!

10. No, don't worry about the money; it's ....no object..................... - whatever it costs, I'll pay.

11. If you're so confident in what you're saying, why don't you put your money, you know, ...where your mouth is.... ?

12. We finally got the deal done when I offered him an extra four hundred a week - ....money talks................. !

DOWN

1. We got the forest fire under control just ....in the nick of time...... ; it was about to engulf that house there.

2. Look at the way he behaves so carelessly with his money; you'd think he had ....money to burn............ .

3. Don't worry, I'll clean up the mess. There's no need to get upset; I don't like to see people .....cry over spilt milk..... .

5. It took us weeks to finalise the deal. In the end, I ....met him halfway..................... , so he got some of what he wanted and so did I - we were both fairly happy!

IDIOMS

bear something in mind	in your right mind	slip someone's mind
blow someone's mind	have a mind of your own	mind over matter
change your mind	make up your mind	speak your mind
cross someone's mind	mind you	great minds think alike

bear something in mind (or bear in mind something) - remember something or take it into consideration.
Bear in mind that it could rain every day, even in the middle of the summer - that's the downside of a holiday in Ireland.

blow someone's mind - to surprise, amaze or excite someone greatly.
It blows my mind to think that people built these monuments over five thousand years ago.

change your mind - change your opinion, or change a decision or choice that you have made.
I thought that she was quite nice at first, but I've changed my mind now after getting to know her a little better.

cross someone's mind - If a thought crosses your mind, you think about it for a moment.
It crossed my mind recently that I haven't heard from Nick for a long time; I wonder what he's doing.

in your right mind - A person is in their right mind if they are in a normal mental state; if they are sane as opposed to mad.
I know she said some terrible things, but she wasn't in her right mind. She has just lost her job, Tim; she is depressed.

have a mind of your own - You talk about a person or animal having a mind of their own if they are able to think for themselves, and do not accept other people's instructions or opinions without question. Saying someone has a mind of their own can also mean they are very independent.
She won't be influenced by what her friends decide to do; Rachel's got a mind of her own and she'll go to Africa by herself if she wants to.

make up your mind - make a decision or form an opinion.
I'd like to come, but I may not have time. Can I phone you back when I've made up my mind?

mind you - People say "mind you" as a way of emphasising a point, especially a new point which has not previously or recently been mentioned.
The food at the cafe is very good. Mind you, it isn't cheap.

slip someone's mind - forget to do something, or forget to deal with it.
A: "Have you phoned the bank yet?"
B: "Oh, I'm sorry. It completely slipped my mind."

mind over matter - If people talk about mind over matter, they mean the power that determination can give you to succeed in something which you may have thought you were physically unable to do; in other words, mind over matter means that if you are determined enough, you can succeed in a difficult task (it doesn't necessarily have to be a physical task, it can be a mental one, too).
I kept telling myself it was just a case of mind over matter as I struggled on slowly up towards the top of the mountain.

speak your mind - say what you really think.
I'm going to tell that nasty little man exactly what I think of him. I'm not afraid to speak my mind.

great minds think alike - If someone says "great minds think alike", they mean that clever people usually agree or have the same ideas and opinions.
A: "I was just about to say that myself."
B: "Great minds think alike, eh?"

A. Fill in the gaps in the sentences below with the correct Idiom from Unit 9.

1. One minute it's raining; the next it's bright and sunny. I wish the weather would .....make up its mind...... .

2. Rachel was known to change her mind a lot; ...mind you, when she eventually made a decision she would fully commit.

3. Come on Rebecca, I know it's difficult but you can recover from this illness; ....mind over matter..... , remember.

4. .....Bear in mind. that these pyramids were built thousands of years ago; amazing, isn't it?

5. The thought of what his son Max might be doing in America often .....crossed.... Paul's .....mind....... .

6. No one .in their right mind. would believe me if I told them that I just saw two dogs; one standing on top of the other!

7. It's only 9 o'clock. If you ..change your mind.. we still have time to drive to the concert venue. What do you think?

8. I'm really sorry Sarah. I know you asked me to stop off at the supermarket for milk, but it just ..slipped my mind.. .

9. Des decided to .....speak his mind... to Nancy and tell her exactly what he thought of her disappointing behaviour.

10. I was surprised that Nicola liked the food so much; she said the taste really ..blew her mind.. .

11. Mike's friends had all gone to the party together, but he had ..a mind of his own.. , so he went for a run instead.

12. Of course we all got the same answer; I'm not a bit surprised. After all, ...great minds think alike... .

B. Choose the correct answer **A, B, C** or **D**.

13. Oh, that daughter of mine never listens to anything I say. She'll just do what she wants anyway; ....
    a. she bears it in mind
    b. she changes her mind
    c. she has a mind of her own
    d. she makes up her mind

14. **A:** "Do you believe in love at first sight?"
    B: "I haven't .... about that yet."
    a. made up my mind
    b. been in my right mind
    c. changed my mind
    d. slipped my mind

15. You know what they say; although .... , fools seldom differ!
    a. bear in mind
    b. in your right mind
    c. mind over matter
    d. great minds think alike

16. .... that your poor grandad is getting old, Len. He can't play with you for as long as he used.
    a. Great minds think alike
    b. Bear in mind
    c. Cross your mind
    d. Mind you

17. You would have to pay me a lot of money to do something so stupid as that. .... , £1m would do!
    a. Cross your mind
    b. Change your mind
    c. Make up your mind
    d. Mind you

18. That lecture in physics yesterday really .... Who would have guessed the atom could be so amazing?
    a. had a mind of its own
    b. crossed my mind
    c. slipped my mind
    d. blew my mind

19. It almost .... , but don't worry, I remembered to pick up some cookies for you on the way home!
    a. crossed my mind
    b. blew my mind
    c. slipped my mind
    d. made up my mind

20. If you .... one more time, I'll make this decision for you!
    a. change your mind
    b. have a mind of your own
    c. make up your mind
    d. place mind over matter

21. Come on! Let's do this; you know we can. All it takes is a little bit of .... and we'll reach the top.
    a. great minds thinking alike
    b. mind over matter
    c. speaking your mind
    d. blowing your mind

22. You know, until you mentioned it, the thought hadn't ....
    a. changed my mind
    b. crossed my mind
    c. slipped my mind
    d. been in my right mind

23. You're not .... Mary; you need to go and see a doctor before this becomes serious.
    a. in your right mind
    b. blowing my mind
    c. speaking your mind
    d. mind you

24. I admire people who just .... no matter what the consequences of being honest are.
    a. mind you
    b. slip their mind
    c. speak their mind
    d. are in their right mind

C. Match the Definitions with the correct Idiom. There are 3 extra Idioms that do not match with any Definition.

25. Keep it under consideration.

26. Excite you greatly.

27. Alter your decision.

28. If you think about it briefly it will...

29. Sane and able to think clearly.

30. Be very independent in the way you think.

31. Decide something.

32. A way of emphasising a new point.

33. To forget to do something is to let it...

34. Determination to get the task done even though it's difficult.

35. Say what you think.

36. Clever people have similar ideas.

25.	n
26.	c
27.	f
28.	g
29.	d
30.	o
31.	m
32.	b
33.	a
34.	e
35.	l
36.	i

a. slip your mind

b. mind you

c. blow your mind

d. in your right mind

e. mind over matter

f. change your mind

g. cross your mind

h. call it a day

i. great minds think alike

j. look daggers

k. come in from the cold

l. speak your mind

m. make up your mind

n. bear it in mind

o. have a mind of your own

D. Fill in the gaps with the correct Idiom.

"(37) Great minds think alike ", my old physics professor would always say to me. But I'm not so sure; I think smart people tend to disagree with each other more often than not! Maybe that's me speaking from personal experience because I'm very argumentative myself and always (38) speak my mind . You might say that's a bad quality, but I respect honesty in a person. It has never, not even once in these past forty years (39) crossed my mind not to say what I really think. After all, what's the point in lying to people? (40) Mind you , I'm sure it makes life easier! I know I've gotten into a lot of trouble over the years for saying what I really think. But who cares! You only live once.

But getting back to my old science professor, apart from my disagreeing with his reasoning for why some people tend to agree, I have to admit we actually had a lot in common. He did what he wanted and decided things for himself; he had (41) a mind of his own just like me, I suppose. And he was stubborn, too. It was impossible to (42) change his mind ; once he'd decided to do something, that was it! I have to admit I'm not as clever as him though. His intellect would sometimes (43) blow my mind ; it was phenomenal.

I am just as forgetful as he was, though, that's for sure! The professor was terrible for letting things (44) slip his mind . He would forget to bring books to class, return assignments to the students - the list goes on and on. Some people used to question whether or not he was (45) in his right mind ; such was his forgetfulness. But I never did. I admired him greatly. (46) Bear in mind he was 75 years old and he was still more interesting than all the other lecturers on our course. I can't (47) make up my mind if I found him so interesting because he clearly loved physics or because I do - maybe it was a combination of both.

Uh! Chemistry was a different story though - I hated it. But, (48) mind over matter as they say; I worked hard and got the best grade in my class despite my lack of interest in the subject.

E. Do the CrossWord Puzzle, finding the correct IDIOM from Unit 9.

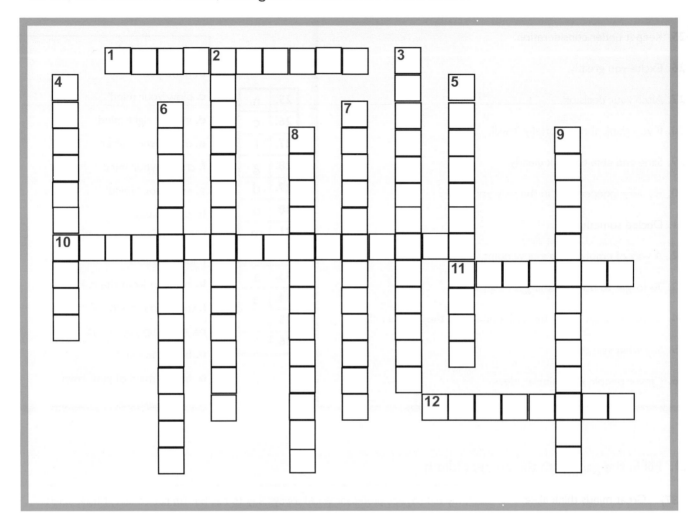

ACROSS

1. His story was so inspiring; it just totally ....blew my mind........... .

10. No one ......in their right mind..... would attempt a such a dangerous jump from Niagara Falls.

11. I don't think I did very well in that test. ....Mind you... , neither did anyone else by the looks on their faces!

12. Oh! I think this computer ....has a mind.......... of its own; it just seems to do whatever it wants!

DOWN

2. ......Mind over matter...... , they kept saying to me, but I just couldn't physically do it, so I gave up.

3. Don't tell me he has finally ....made up his mind... to go to Australia; he's been talking about doing that for years!

4. Of course we agree! You know what they say about ....great minds....... , don't you? They always think alike.

5. It can't have ......slipped.......... my .....mind..... ; I'm sure you just forgot to say it to me.

6. He didn't realise you had those feelings for him; the thought hadn't ..crossed his mind....... once.

7. A: "It's going to be a lot colder in Finland; you'd better pack some extra layers in your hand luggage to put on when you get there."   **B:** "I'll ....bear it in mind........... ."

8. You haven't ....changed my mind.... ; I'm still going to quit my job so there's no point trying to convince me to do otherwise.

9. You're among friends here. Please, don't be afraid to ....speak your mind....... .

UNIT 10

IDIOMS

down in the mouth	**music to someone's ears**	**odd one out**
foam at the mouth	your nearest and dearest	against all odds
get on someone's nerves	**a nip in the air**	**at odds with**
face the music	nip and tuck	as of now

down in the mouth - Someone who is down in the mouth is feeling sad.
He had never seen Karl looking so down in the mouth. "Cheer up", he said. "It can't be that bad."

foam at the mouth - to be mad with anger; to be very very angry.
He scares me a little. One minute he's foaming at the mouth and the next he's laughing and joking - I can never tell which Paul I am going to see.

get on someone's nerves - annoys or irritate someone a lot.
That dripping tap is getting on my nerves. Why haven't you called the plumber yet?

face the music - You face the music when you put yourself into an unpleasant situation involving strong criticism of your past actions, where you will have to either admit that you were wrong or defend what you have done; or when you make a decision to accept and deal with the punishment, criticism or negative response that you think your past actions will result in.
Jenny has a right to be angry with you, and the longer you leave it before you speak to her, the worse it will get. Why don't you just face the music now?

music to someone's ears - If it gives you great pleasure to hear something - good news, for example - you can say that that thing is music to your ears.
A: "I'll do the washing-up, shall I?"
B: "Ah, that's music to my ears."

your nearest and dearest - your closest family and friends; your loved ones.
By writing a proper will in advance of your passing, you will save your nearest and dearest from paying an unnecessary amount of inheritance tax.

a nip in the air - If you say that there is a nip in the air, you mean that the weather is a bit cold.
There was a nip in the air; winter was only just round the corner.

nip and tuck - If a competition is described as nip and tuck, it is so close that you do not know who will win; if you describe the outcome of a situation which will either result in success or failure as nip and tuck, you mean it is not yet very clear which outcome will come to be.
As the horses rounded the last bend, it was still nip and tuck.

odd one out - Someone or something that is the odd one out in any group is the one that is noticeably different from the rest.
Look at these objects and tell me which is the odd one out.

against all odds - Something happens, is done or succeeds against all odds, when it happens, is done or succeeds despite great difficulty or disadvantage; when it succeeds even though there was only a very small possibility of success at the beginning.
Against all odds, I somehow escaped from the avalanche by riding the top of the wave of snow on my skis.

at odds with - You are at odds with someone when you are in disagreement with or in opposition to them.
How can we ever agree when his views are at odds with everything I believe in?

as of now - starting from now; from this moment onwards; beginning now.
As of now, all goods must be paid for in cash at the time of purchase.

Illustrated English Idioms

A. Fill in the gaps in the sentences below with the correct Idiom from Unit 10.

1. A: "Do you think Paul looks a little down in the mouth ?"
B: "A little! I'd say he looks pretty devastated, poor fellow!

4. I'm absolutely foaming at the mouth . How dare they charge me £5,000 to fix a tiny scratch to the paintwork on my car?

2. Stop freezing!! This computer is so slow that it's really ....getting on my nerves...... . Ugh! Come on; hurry up!

5. You've really done it now; dad is foaming at the mouth; prepare to ..face the music............. !

3. John counts his dog, Judge, among his very nearest and dearest friends. I'm sure Tobby feels the same!

6. The news that there would soon be another member of the family was ...music to their ears.... ; they couldn't wait!

7. Brrrr! There's a real ....nip.in.the.air....... today; it feels almost cold enough to snow, I'd say.

8. Hands up; who can spot which one is the ...odd.one.out.. ? I'll give you a clue; he's the centre of attention!

9. Jane and Simon were still ..at.odds.with..... each other over who should be the one to have the T.V. remote control.

10. "And it's .....nip.and.tuck...... all the way to the finish line, but Sunshine Runner takes it by a head."

11. ....As.of.now...., I have decided never to sleep on a hammock between two large rocks ever again.

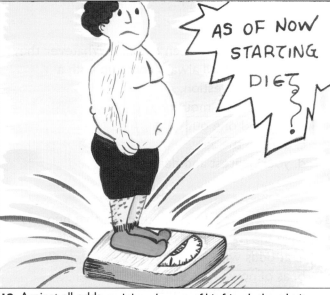

12. Against.all.odds, and though none of his friends thought it possible, he managed to lose 20 pounds in less than a month.

B. Choose the correct answer **A**, **B**, **C** or **D**.

13. It's certainly strange weather for late Spring; there's ....
    a. an odd one out
    b. music to my ears
    c. quite a nip in the air
    d. nothing, as of now

14. .... , I am officially the new Managing Director of Stork Primrose Enterprises.
    a. Foaming at the mouth
    b. Your nearest and dearest
    c. As of now
    d. It's nip and tuck

15. .... , he managed to crawl his way down the mountain with a broken leg and two crushed ribs.
    a. Nip and tuck
    b. Against all odds
    c. As of now
    d. Facing the music

16. It was .... there for a while, but, in the end, I managed to get just ahead to claim victory.
    a. nip and tuck
    b. the odd one out
    c. music to my ears
    d. getting on my nerves

17. James has always been .... Whatever they want to do, he'll always come up with a different suggestion.
    a. down in the mouth
    b. the odd one out
    c. a nip in the air
    d. your nearest and dearest

18. I have always felt .... the idea that humans have the right to do lab tests on animals.
    a. at odds with
    b. as of now
    c. foaming at the mouth
    d. like facing the music with

19. Ever since he and Kathy split up, he's been a bit .... I feel sorry for him.
    a. down in the mouth
    b. the odd one out
    c. nip and tuck
    d. against all odds

20. It's so nice to see .... here with me today.
    a. the odd one out
    b. all of my nearest and dearest
    c. a nip in the air
    d. someone getting on my nerves

21. I made a really big mistake and now I'm going to have to pay for it; it's time to ....
    a. be music to my ears
    b. be at odds with
    c. foam at the mouth
    d. face the music

22. You're getting married! Oh, wonderful; that's .... I'm thrilled for both of you.
    a. facing the music
    b. your nearest and dearest
    c. as of now
    d. music to my ears

23. When I learned that my 'supposed' best friend had betrayed me, I was ....
    a. nip and tuck
    b. foaming at the mouth
    c. getting on my nerves
    d. facing the music

24. Don't click your knuckles like that; it really .... - what a horrible sound!
    a. foams at the mouth
    b. gets on my nerves
    c. is the odd one out
    d. is against all odds

C. Match the Definitions with the correct Idiom. There are 3 extra Idioms that do not match with any Definition.

25. Feeling very sad.

26. Starting from this moment.

27. If you are in disagreement with someone, you are .... them.

28. Very angry.

29. Achieved despite great difficulty and despite there being little prospect of success in the beginning; achieved...

30. Really irritating someone.

31. Different from all the rest.

32. Deal with the negative reaction to your actions.

33. Close all the way to the finish.

34. News which you welcome enthusiastically is...

35. Your closest friends and people you love the most.

36. It is noticeably cold, so there is...

25.	e
26.	f
27.	m
28.	i
29.	a
30.	h
31.	n
32.	o
33.	b
34.	c
35.	k
36.	l

a. against all odds

b. nip and tuck

c. music to your ears

d. change your mind

e. down in the mouth

f. as of now

g. slip someone's mind

h. getting on someone's nerves

i. foaming at the mouth

j. mind over matter

k. your nearest and dearest

l. a nip in the air

m. at odds with

n. the odd one out

o. face the music

D. Fill in the gaps with the correct Idiom.

Michael and I have been (37)................at odds with.......... one another ever since we had a big disagreement over who should organise Tom's birthday party. Needless to say, I am quite (38).......down in the mouth..... about it because, untill now, we have always been the best of friends. In fact, I would have always counted Michael among my (39)......nearest and dearest...... .

(40)...............As of now................. , I will try to make things better - you see I can't help but feel a bit like the (41).........odd one out............... because everyone else gets on with him so well. Perhaps it's my fault and I should just apologise to him and (42).....face the music............. . We said some harsh words to one another, so I'm sure he will be very critical of me, but I have to deal with the problem soon if I want to save our friendship. It's going to be (43)..............nip and tuck.............. - I am by no means sure what the outcome of our discussion will be, but I am hopeful the memory of our years of friendship together will win out over his current anger.

We've never before (44).got on each other's nerves.. so much, so it is strange to think how irritated we feel in each other's company these days. In fact, the more I think about it, the less confident I am that I can rescue the situation, but I'm hoping I will be able to do just that (45).........against all odds............ .

There's a real (46)...........nip in the air.... today as a cold northerly wind has blown in overnight. But the air is fresh and clean as a consequence - maybe that bodes well for a fresh start for me, too. I called him to arrange a clear-the-air meeting. I really hope he doesn't charge into the room (47)..foaming at the mouth..... , still angry with me for what I've said and done. But, should he accept my apology, that would simply be (48)......music to my ears........... .

E. Do the CrossWord Puzzle, finding the correct IDIOM from Unit 10.

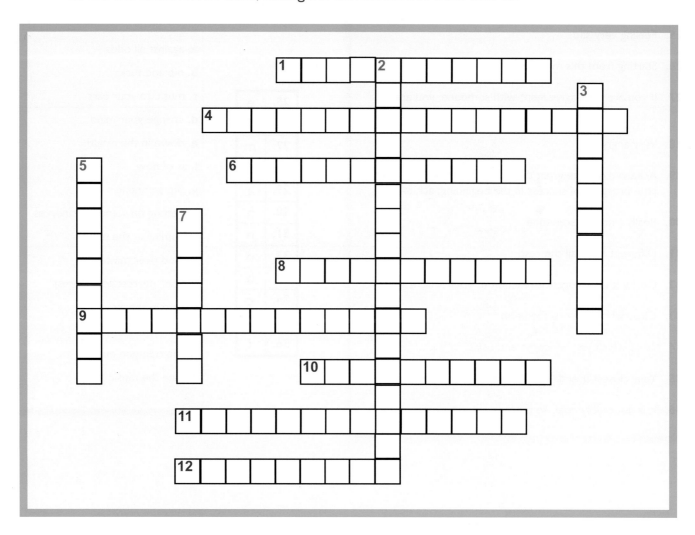

ACROSS

1. Be quiet, will you? You're really beginning to ..get on.... my ..nerves...... .
4. Calm down! You're absolutely ....foaming at the mouth............. . What happened to make you so worked up?
6. He squandered all his money and now he's got to ....face the music.................... .
8. Put your coat on before you go out; there's a real ....nip in the air......................... .
9. ....Against all odds............... , we had a snowstorm in late June.
10. It was ....nip and tuck...................... as to which car would pass the finish line first.
11. He has been a bit ....down in the mouth............. ever since he learned that he didn't get the job.
12. I am the ....odd one out.................... amongst my friends; I'm single and all the rest of them are married.

DOWN

2. You may wish to inform those who are ....nearest and dearest...........to you of the possibility that you may not return from this mission.
3. The opposition is ....at odds with.................... the government again over the proposed reform of the Land Act.
5. When my numbers came up in last night's lottery draw, it was .....music............... to my ....ears...... .
7. ....As of now...................... , there is a new procedure for dealing with customer complaints; please read the memo.

Revision Test

2

Units 6-10

A. Match the first half of the sentence with the second half containing the correct Idiom

1. Apparently, the rumour about him being a convict was

2. When he asked me to marry him, I was

3. I think you should be careful how many sick days you take. Don't

4. I will not accept anything less than full payment and that's

5. You should ask for a promotion

6. She is his second cousin, once removed, to

7. Despite a six-week-long investigation, the police couldn't

8. Stop acting like a baby! There's no point in

9. Mark, wearing that bright pink shirt

10. That guy is crazy. If I ever see him again I am going to

11. I can't afford to buy you that computer game. I don't

12. That experience you had in Malaysia sounds amazing; it must have really

13. If you think I am going to pay for the damage you caused you can't be

14. Tell me exactly what you want to say. Don't be afraid to

15. I'm disappointed you decided not to come, but don't be afraid to

16. Surely we're witnessing a superstar

17. Well, it's a shame we don't have enough cups for everyone, but I suppose we'll have to

18. Trust me, if you work hard enough, you will definitely

19. I got transferred into the I.T. department yesterday. My first role helped me get there; it was just

20. He's unbelievably rich, so you can name your price because

1.	i
2.	m
3.	h
4.	b
5.	d
6.	r
7.	t
8.	p
9.	o
10	e
11	q
12	k
13.	j
14.	f
15.	a
16.	l
17.	g
18.	s
19.	n
20.	c

a. change your mind.

b. the bottom line.

c. money is no object.

d. in light of your good performance.

e. run a mile.

f. speak your mind.

g. make do.

h. push your luck.

i. a load of rubbish.

j. in your right mind.

k. blown your mind.

l. in the making.

m. at a loss for words.

n. a means to an end.

o. you stand out a mile.

p. crying over spilt milk.

q. have money to burn.

r. he best of my knowledge.

s. make it.

t. cast any light on what happened.

B. Write **C** or **I** (**Correct** or **Incorrect**) in the box to the right for each sentence using an Idiom.

21. I completely forgot; it just crossed my mind.	**21.** I
22. I can't seem to control this car at all; it's like it has a mind of its own.	**22.** C
23. They are entering into money talks today.	**23.** I
24. I arrived just in the nick of time for the start of the performance.	**24.** C
25. Now that we are here, we might as well make the most of it.	**25.** C
26. By all means pour me another glass; I'd love one!	**26.** C
27. You spend too much money; that's why you can't live beyond your means.	**27.** I
28. Jane was very quick off the mark, so she arrived five hours late.	**28.** I
29. Have you lost you marbles or something Tom? I'm beginning to worry about you!	**29.** C
30. It's great to see you looking so down in the mouth again.	**30.** I
31. You can't avoid her forever; you'll have to face the music sooner or later!	**31.** C
32. This is going to be a small party - I'm only inviting our nearest and dearest friends.	**32.** C
33. You passed! Ah, that's simply fantastic; music to my ears!	**33.** C
34. He barely makes a sound when he enters the room; he's larger than life.	**34.** I
35. I like his plays; they're very true to life, don't you think?	**35.** C
36. Tough luck. At least you played your best; that's all you can do.	**36.** C
37. Ever since he got promoted, he's really made his mark - a terrific contribution.	**37.** C
38. Your acceptance of me into the group means a lot. I feel like the odd one out.	**38.** I
39. As of now, the new dress code is in force; formal clothing at all times.	**39.** C
40. Oh, that was quite lucky; I almost slipped my mind and hit my head.	**40.** I

C. Fill in the gaps in the text with the correct form of the **Idioms** from the box below.

use your loaf	meet someone	bear something in mind	mind you
step out of line	halfway	at odds with	make up your mind
make it up	foam at the mouth	against all odds	leave a mark
within your means	get on someone's	nip and tuck	put your money where your mouth is
the more the merrier	nerves	a nip in the air	
not to mention	mind over matter	great minds think alike	

Even though it's not yet winter, there was definitely (41) .....a nip in the air..... when I left for work this morning. (42) .....Mind you..... , at least it's not raining anymore. Last week we had monsoon-like rain, (43) .....not to mention..... flooding, which caused quite a lot of damage.

I am really looking forward to finishing work tonight; the staff Christmas party is on afterwards. In fact, I'm finding it hard to concentrate on what I have to do today, as I'm so excited about the big event. But, (44) .....mind over matter..... , I'll just have to focus on working hard for another few hours even though the stuff I'm doing is dead boring!

My girlfriend, Sarah, is coming tonight. Last year, I had to work over Christmas, so she was really upset with me. But this time I'm going to (45) .....make it up..... to her - we're flying out to Rovaniemi in Lapland for the Christmas week for a very special festive season. I (46) .....made up my mind..... to book Rovaniemi just yesterday. It was either going to be there or Saint Petersburg - it was (47) .....nip and tuck..... until the last minute to decide which one would win in my mind!

I'll be glad to get away from the office for a week. One of the other members of staff is really beginning to (48) .....get on my nerves..... . He keeps saying he's better than me at everything. '(49) .....Put your money where your mouth is..... and let's have a bet on who gets the bigger Christmas bonus', I said to him - I really hope I win! I suggested a bet of £100; he suggested £50. In the end, he (50) .....met me halfway..... at £75.

Everyone in the office is talking about it, and if he loses, it'll (51) .....leave a mark..... on his ego for a very long time. He's not a bad fellow really; we always just seem to be (52) .....at odds with..... one another. We can never agree on anything - I suppose it's some sort of male rivalry.

I really could do with a big bonus as well. I'm not long out of college and haven't yet learned to live (53) .....within my means..... . As a consequence, I'm always deeply in debt. I've been thinking with my wallet, too much - I need to start (54) .....using my loaf..... instead from now on! (55) .....Bear in mind..... I'm only earning the minimum wage though; it's not easy to survive on that let me tell you.

If I don't get a nice big Christmas bonus, I'll be (56) .....foaming at the mouth..... . I've worked my guts out and I really think I deserve it. I never (57) .....step out of line..... and I always do as I'm asked; I'm an honest, hard worker. Compare that with Dave - the guy I made the bet with. Dave is lazy and incompetent; if he gets a bigger bonus than me it will be (58) .....against all odds..... . The only thing he's good at is sucking up to the boss. He agrees with everything the boss says; no questions asked. (59) .....Great minds think alike..... - yeah right! More like lazy workers say 'yes' to every idea the boss has. But I'm glad I made this bet with him. I welcome healthy competition - (60) .....the more the merrier..... , I say!

So bring it on Dave! You have £75 with my name written on it!

Idioms Index

a fool and his money are soon parted (unit 2)
a frog in your throat (unit 2)
a load of rubbish (unit 6)
a means to an end (unit 7)
a nip in the air (unit 10)
a/some kind of (unit 4)
against all odds (unit 10)
as of now (unit 10)
at a loss (unit 6)
at large (unit 5)
at odds with (unit 10)

be/step out of line (unit 6)
bear something in mind (unit 9)
beyond a joke (unit 4)
beyond your means (unit 7)
blow someone's mind (unit 9)
break new ground (unit 3)
bring someone to their knees (unit 4)
by all means (unit 7)

cast (some) light on something (unit 6)
change your mind (unit 9)
cross someone's mind (unit 9)
cry over spilt milk (unit 8)

down in the mouth (unit 10)
drag your feet (unit 1)

face the music (unit 10)
fair and square (unit 1)
feather in your cap (unit 1)
fingers crossed (unit 1)
flash in the pan (unit 1)
foam at the mouth (unit 10)
fools rush in (unit 2)
for a start (unit 4)

get cold feet (unit 1)
get off on the wrong foot (unit 2)
get on someone's nerves (unit 10)
get to grips with (unit 3)
give 'em an inch and they'll take a mile (unit 4)
give as good as you get (unit 2)
give someone a free hand (unit 3)
go to great lengths (unit 5)
great minds think alike (unit 9)
grin and bear it (unit 2)

hand in glove (unit 3)
have a mind of your own (unit 9)
have money to burn (unit 8)
have the guts to do something (unit 3)
have your hands full (unit 3)

hit the jackpot (unit 4)
hold the fort (unit 2)
hold your ground (unit 3)

in light of (unit 6)
in the least (unit 5)
in the making (unit 7)
in the nick of time (unit 8)
in your right mind (unit 9)

keep up with the Joneses (unit 5)
keep your hair on (unit 3)
knock it off (unit 5)

larger than life (unit 6)
last but not least (unit 5)
leave someone standing (unit 5)
leave your/a mark (unit 7)
(not) let the grass grow under your feet (unit 2)
let it drop (unit 5)
let it slip (unit 5)
lose face (unit 1)
lose your marbles (unit 7)

make do (unit 7)
make it (unit 7)
make it up (unit 7)
make the best of a bad job (unit 4)
make the grade (unit 2)
make the most of something (unit 8)
make up your mind (unit 9)
make your mark (unit 7)
meet someone halfway (unit 8)
mind over matter (unit 9)
mind you (unit 9)
money is no object (unit 8)
money talks (unit 8)
music to someone's ears (unit 10)

nip and tuck (unit 10)
no kidding? (unit 4)
not to mention (unit 8)

odd one out (unit 10)
of a kind (unit 4)
old hand (unit 3)
on hand (unit 3)
open the floodgates (unit 1)

push your luck (unit 6)
put your foot down (unit 2)
put your money where your mouth is (unit 8)

quick off the mark (unit 7)

run a mile (unit 8)

save face (unit 1)
slip someone's mind (unit 9)
speak your mind (unit 9)
stand out a mile (unit 8)

take a joke (unit 4)
take your fancy (unit 1)
that figures (unit 1)
the bottom line (unit 6)
the fast lane (unit 5)
the grass is always greener on the other side (unit 2)
the kiss of death (unit 4)
the more the merrier (unit 8)
tie the knot (unit 5)
to the best of your knowledge (unit 6)
to the letter (unit 5)
tough luck (unit 6)
true to life (unit 6)

under the knife (unit 4)
up to no good (unit 2)
use your loaf (unit 6)

win hands down (unit 3)
within your means (unit 7)
work your fingers to the bone (unit 1)
work your guts out (unit 3)

your nearest and dearest (unit 10)

Irregular Verbs Index

Base Form	Simple Past	Past Participle
awake	awoke	awoken
be	was, were	been
bear	bore	born
beat	beat	beaten
become	became	become
begin	began	begun
bend	bent	bent
beset	beset	beset
bet	bet	bet
bid	bid/bade	bid/bidden
bind	bound	bound
bite	bit	bitten
bleed	bled	bled
blow	blew	blown
break	broke	broken
breed	bred	bred
bring	brought	brought
broadcast	broadcast	broadcast
build	built	built
burn	burned/burnt	burned/burnt
burst	burst	burst
buy	bought	bought
cast	cast	cast
catch	caught	caught
choose	chose	chosen
cling	clung	clung
come	came	come
cost	cost	cost
creep	crept	crept
cut	cut	cut
deal	dealt	dealt
dig	dug	dug
dive	dived/dove	dived
do	did	done
draw	drew	drawn
dream	dreamed/dreamt	dreamed/dreamt
drive	drove	driven
drink	drank	drunk
eat	ate	eaten
fall	fell	fallen
feed	fed	fed
feel	felt	felt
fight	fought	fought
find	found	found
fit	fit	fit
flee	fled	fled
fling	flung	flung
fly	flew	flown
forbid	forbade	forbidden
forget	forgot	forgotten
forego (forgo)	forewent	foregone
forgive	forgave	forgiven
forsake	forsook	forsaken
freeze	froze	frozen
get	got	got/gotten
give	gave	given
go	went	gone
grind	ground	ground
grow	grew	grown
hang	hung	hung
hear	heard	heard
hide	hid	hidden
hit	hit	hit
hold	held	held
hurt	hurt	hurt
keep	kept	kept
kneel	knelt	knelt
knit	knit	knit
know	knew	known
lay	laid	laid
lead	led	led
leap	leaped/leapt	leaped/leapt

Base Form	Simple Past	Past Participle
learn	learned/learnt	learned/learnt
leave	left	left
lend	lent	lent
let	let	let
lie	lay	lain
light	lighted/lit	lighted/lit
lose	lost	lost
make	made	made
mean	meant	meant
meet	met	met
misspell	misspelled/misspelt	misspelled/misspelt
mistake	mistook	mistaken
mow	mowed	mowed/mown
overcome	overcame	overcome
overdo	overdid	overdone
overtake	overtook	overtaken
overthrow	overthrew	overthrown
pay	paid	paid
plead	pled	pled
prove	proved	proved/proven
put	put	put
quit	quit	quit
read	read	read
rid	rid	rid
ride	rode	ridden
ring	rang	rung
rise	rose	risen
run	ran	run
saw	sawed	sawed/sawn
say	said	said
see	saw	seen
seek	sought	sought
sell	sold	sold
send	sent	sent
set	set	set
sew	sewed	sewed/sewn
shake	shook	shaken
shave	shaved	shaved/shaven
shear	shore	shorn
shed	shed	shed
shine	shone	shone
shoe	shoed	shoed/shod
shoot	shot	shot
show	showed	showed/shown
shrink	shrank	shrunk
shut	shut	shut
sing	sang	sung
sink	sank	sunk
sit	sat	sat
sleep	slept	slept
slay	slew	slain
slide	slid	slid
sling	slung	slung
slit	slit	slit
smite	smote	smitten
sow	sowed	sowed/sown
speak	spoke	spoken
speed	sped	sped
spend	spent	spent
spill	spilled/spilt	spilled/spilt
spin	spun	spun
spit	spit/spat	spit
split	split	split
spread	spread	spread
spring	sprang/sprung	sprung
stand	stood	stood
steal	stole	stolen
stick	stuck	stuck
sting	stung	stung

Irregular Verbs

Base Form	Simple Past	Past Participle
stink	stank	stunk
stride	strode	stridden
strike	struck	struck
string	strung	strung
strive	strove	striven
swear	swore	sworn
sweep	swept	swept
swell	swelled	swelled/swollen
swim	swam	swum
swing	swung	swung
take	took	taken
teach	taught	taught
tear	tore	torn
tell	told	told
think	thought	thought
thrive	thrived/throve	thrived
throw	threw	thrown
thrust	thrust	thrust
tread	trod	trodden
understand	understood	understood
uphold	upheld	upheld
upset	upset	upset
wake	woke	woken
wear	wore	worn
weave	weaved/wove	weaved/woven
wed	wed	wed
weep	wept	wept
wind	wound	wound
win	won	won
withhold	withheld	withheld
withstand	withstood	withstood
wring	wrung	wrung
write	wrote	written